COMPUTERS
ON
CAMPUS

NOTE ON AUTHORS

The senior author of this report, John Caffrey, now director of the Commission on Administrative Affairs, was, at the time this study was designed and conducted and while most of the report was being written, Program Director for Education, Advanced Systems Division, System Development Corporation, and principal investigator for the project. The junior author, Charles Mosmann, is a staff associate in the same division of System Development Corporation.

JOHN CAFFREY
CHARLES J. MOSMANN

with illustrations by
ROBERT OSBORN

COMPUTERS ON CAMPUS

*A Report to the President
on Their Use and Management*

AMERICAN COUNCIL ON EDUCATION,
WASHINGTON, D.C.

FOREWORD

UNLIKE PROFESSORS, who may rise to fame by knowing a great deal about one subject, academic administrators must know at least something about a lot of different things. The computer is one of the many things they need to know about these days. *Computers on Campus* is designed to supply the kind of basic knowledge needed by those who make policy decisions regarding the abuses and uses of this spectacular invention. Not intended for experts, this is a non-technical report. It is designed for generalists whose decisions influence the behavior of specialists. Others may read it with profit, but it is addressed primarily to principal administrators of colleges and universities.

The task of college and university administration is today one of unprecedented complexity. It cannot be made easy by the computer or any other mechanical device, but the computer is not only an object of growing interest to scholars and scientists but also an aid to administrators in decision-making. For many educational leaders, however, the computer is an arcane rather than a familiar instrument. To help them understand what this piece of machinery is and what it can do on their campuses, the American Council on Education and the College Entrance Examination Board sponsored the study that resulted in this book. Dividends from our substantial investment can be realized only if the findings and recommendations of the study are noted by presidents and others and then brought to bear on relevant campus problems.

This report is in several respects an unusual one for the Council. Its subject matter is more technical than that of most of our publications, many of which are intended for persons who know a lot about the matters under discussion; this one makes no such assumption about its intended readers. Although it has some things to say to administrators who are already experienced in problems of the insti-

v

tutional management of computer installations, it can be understood by the individual who has never even seen a machine. Its intent is to clarify some major issues and to give the president a background against which to make decisions about the uses to be made of this increasingly important device on his own campus.

Another unusual aspect of this report is that the Council staff had a very minor role in its preparation; we obtained the services of a nonprofit research and development agency, the System Development Corporation. They designed and executed the study. This firm was chosen because of its wide experience in dealing with the subject at hand and also because it had no hardware to sell and, indeed, nothing to gain from any position of advocacy.

As the reader will note, the book specifies that many problems can be solved and many systems improved without the use of computers. One purpose of this report is to assist the administrator in differentiating between the legitimate need for computer services and promotional efforts to further the use of what has become a prestigious mechanism in some academic circles.

For some years to come many institutions will not be able or ready to make the financial and other commitments necessary to keep pace with the computer revolution. Some colleges, for example, may wisely place the computer on a lower priority rating than improved salary scales, residential housing, library expansion, and other needed changes. Even in impoverished places, however, there doubtless will be the temptation to think that the addition of sophisticated automated devices and systems will per se solve problems. Central to this report, and to the thinking which led to its sponsorship by the Council, is the conviction that any action should be preceded by a careful examination of the important technical variables in the context of local situations.

As I have stated, this inquiry also brings forth some knowledge which will be useful to administrators of institutions which already are making extensive use of computers. One of the findings of the investigation is that the computer does not necessarily become better understood by administrators simply because one or more of these machines have been on the campus for some years. Complacency can be an obstacle to improvement and progress if it is thought that relevant problems have been solved merely by the acquisition of a computer. The opposite error, of course, is the assumption that such an acquisition is unnecessary, irrelevant, or not feasible. This report draws attention to problems which even the administrator of a well-developed automated system may have ignored or underestimated.

It would be presumptuous to hold that this little volume answers all of the important questions any administrative officer may want to ask; indeed, the study does not even answer all of the questions it raises or implies. One of its emphases is on the importance of knowing what questions to ask, how the answers may be evaluated, and what issues must be resolved. In different colleges and universities, as in other administrative organizations, varying circumstances may warrant different answers to the same question. The report provides no ready-made guide for specific procedures.

The Council appreciates the financial assistance and advice of the College Entrance Examination Board in the preparation of this report. The report's authors suggest that the reader who feels confident that he understands all of the facts and issues involved in the use and management of computers on today's campus might find it worthwhile to read the last chapter ("In Other Words") first. This chapter summarizes many of the important points in the body of the text. If "In Other Words" elicits any surprises or puzzlement, then even the experienced reader may find that he indeed has something to learn by reviewing the text.

Logan Wilson, *President*
American Council on Education

February 1967

PREFACE

COMPUTERS ARE NOW USED widely in colleges and universities. Continued and rapid future growth is expected. This report presents an analysis of some of the problems and issues associated with computer applications which should be of concern to the academic administrator. The use of the computer as an aid in administration is discussed, as well as the administrative problems involved in the development, establishment, and management of various kinds of college and university computing centers.

The study reported here was conducted by specialists from System Development Corporation, under the combined aegis of the American Council on Education and the College Entrance Examination Board, during the spring and summer of 1966. The study was originally conceived by Edward L. Katzenbach, Jr., then Director of the Council's Commission on Administrative Affairs, because of his interest in the increasing need for college presidents and their staffs to understand the potential of the computer as an aid to administration. The study was later broadened to include those nonadministrative uses of computers which are nevertheless of concern to the president because of the necessity for him to make important and often long-lasting decisions about computers, some of them involving large sums of money and many members of the college staff.

Those conducting the study were experienced in the uses of computers in a variety of applications. Because there is some literature in the subject area, an attempt was made to avoid repeating what has already been said elsewhere, except when essential to the study. The basic approach was to make field visits to campuses in every section of the nation. More than fifty colleges and universities were visited—public and private, large and small, urban and rural. Visits were not confined to those institutions that already have a long accumulated experience with computers.

In addition to visits to centers and laboratories, interviews were conducted with some 250 persons—presidents and other officers, as well as instructors, librarians, and research and computer technical personnel. Sites for visits were selected on the basis of the personal knowledge of the visiting team, on reports of institutions which were reputed to have done something special, or in response to invitations from colleges and universities who heard about the study and kindly invited the team to visit. Unfortunately, limited funds made it impossible to respond to all such invitations.

Because of the highly sensitive nature of many of the discussions, it was early decided (and promised) not to reveal the identity of specific institutions and not even to list them in this report. The interviewers soon discovered that conversations on the subject of computers quickly brought into view many difficult problems of personal relations, campus politics, and controversies among and between those who determine and are affected by educational policies. In cases where the unique nature of the problems encountered might have permitted easy identification, unimportant facts have been altered slightly, but not so as to change the essential lesson to be learned. It is hoped that those who had much of which to be proud will not object to the lack of favorable publicity and that those who shared their problems and worries will not mind being cited so that others can profit from knowing about them—or at least feel consoled that they are not alone in their troubles.

The investigators did not take long to discover that there were many patterns of development, common problems, and similar solutions. The chief sources of differences among situations and systems were the size and source of support of the institution, the historical stage of development of computers on campus, internal politics and personality differences, and varying educational and administrative philosophies.

Inevitably this report will seem dated within a short time, but two continuingly useful conclusions emerge from it. One is that there is great value both to the helper and the helped in exchanging ideas and experiences among institutions with common problems and viewpoints. Indeed, one factor which has accelerated the rapid growth of the whole computer field has been this willingness to share problems and ideas throughout the community. The second is that the kind of study reported here should be made periodically (perhaps on a less ambitious scale), because of the need for academic administrators to be able to assess their own developments and lines of thought in the context of what others have learned and found possible in comparable situations.

It is impossible to name every person who contributed to this study and difficult to thank some of them enough. Visits to most campuses were conducted by the authors; the rest by Einar Stefferud, Robert Filep, Duncan MacQueen, and Richard Williams of System Development Corporation, with additional visits to southern campuses by John Hamblen of the Southern Regional Education Board. Messrs. Stefferud and Filep also contributed materials for part of the text. The authors are grateful for the advice and counsel of an ad hoc advisory committee consisting of Chester Alter, University of Denver; Alexander Astin, American Council on Education; Robert Glover and George Hanford, College Entrance Examination Board; Edward L. Katzenbach, Jr.; Elmo Morgan, University of California; and Sharvy Umbeck, Knox College.

Earlier drafts of this report were reviewed by John Hamblen, G. Truman Hunter of International Business Machines Corporation, and Francis E. Rourke of The Johns Hopkins University; Corol Bok, Harold Borko, Charles Fanwick, and John F. O'Toole, Jr., of the System Development Corporation also reviewed all or parts of the manuscript. The authors wish to express a particular debt of gratitude to Einar Stefferud: his keen understanding of some basic policy problems and his critical sense helped them at numerous key points along their way.

The senior author wishes to express special appreciation to Shirley Harris, System Development Corporation, for her efficiency and devoted assistance during the difficult period of the field surveys and for her painstaking work on reports and manuscripts. The invaluable assistance of Jane Newman, of the Publications Division of the American Council on Education, in the final preparations for publication is gratefully acknowledged.

Particular gratitude is expressed for detailed and helpful comments and suggestions supplied by Fred Vorsanger, Treasurer, American Council on Education; Bruce Partridge, Vice-President for Administration, The Johns Hopkins University; and Howard P. Wile, Executive Secretary, Committee on Governmental Relations of the National Association of College and University Business Officers.

The drawings of Robert Osborn are always a welcome and helpful addition to any exposition, serious or otherwise, and special thanks are due him for his personal interest in this project.

Without exception, the interviewers were impressed by and grateful for the courtesy, hospitality, and candor of the college presidents and their representatives who gave so much of their time to tours and conversations. They were also impressed by the striking ubiquity of some basic problems and by the similarity of solutions and conclusions arrived at from a variety of approaches in different environments.

The interviewers sometimes found themselves being *asked* more questions than were answered by the interviewees. This itself, however, turned out to be very valuable (hopefully to all concerned), because much can be learned from listening to questions. In this, as in any area of problem solving, the forming of good questions is essential to finding good answers.

This report is formally dedicated to those staff members on the visited campuses who answered and asked so many questions.

John Caffrey
Charles J. Mosmann

Washington and Santa Monica
March 1967

CONTENTS

THE COMPUTER AND THE PRESIDENT

MOST COLLEGE[1] PRESIDENTS are not only willing but also unashamed to admit they know very little about computers[2] and computing. The head of one institution said:

All I know about computers is that the people who run them are insatiable. We no sooner uncrate and set up the new one, and the staff tells me it's already obsolete and presents me with a purchase order for the one we ought to have but won't be able to get for another year. As soon as I've approved the hiring of three more programmers I'm told we now have so many we need a supervisor. If the trustees ever ask me how much money we're spending on computers, much less ask me *why*, I'll be speechless.

Many presidents were trained in fields of learning in which the computer either did not, at that time, play an important part or in which the computers then available were very simple and comparatively primitive. The multiple burdens of the presidency are a sufficient reason to protest that time has not allowed them to understand the mysteries, real and imaginary, of computing.

One college president was frank to admit:

I don't even know how much I *should* know about computers. I don't know whether we have too many or too few, or whether we have the right kind, or

---

[1] Throughout most of the discussion, "college" will denote college, university, or other institution of higher education.

[2] In this report, "computer" designates a high-speed, electronic, digital, stored-program computer with magnetic memory device—unless otherwise qualified.

whether we're using them effectively. I'm not sure which are *technical* questions to be solved by experts and which are truly *administrative* ones I should settle. What criteria should I apply to my staff's proposals for action? How can I tell whether my staff is even competent?

At first thought, the willingness of the average administrator to admit he knows little or nothing about computers may be interpreted as a healthy sign of a willingness to learn. On second thought, however, it may be a bad sign. Only rarely do men confess ignorance of something they feel they should know. Hence this apparent humility

may actually reveal the more fundamental view that the subject is *not* one about which they need to feel knowledgeable.

Sooner or later (in most cases sooner than they think), almost all presidents must make decisions regarding the computing facilities of their institutions—acquisition, administration, funding and budgets, policies, services, geographical location on campus, and personnel. Faced with these problems, many presidents feel (often quite correctly) that they are at the mercy of the experts on their staff or from consulting agencies. One president hired a consulting firm to develop a comprehensive plan for his university's computing facilities. When the consultant's recommendations were submitted, the computer center director pointed out with ill-concealed bitterness that he had already made many of these recommendations. The president then said, "I know, but now I understand them."

Compounding the confusions created by the technical problems of data processing and computing, personal and political power struggles may develop around the disposition of computer resources. Control of academic computing facilities may mean personal prestige; more important, the struggle for control may actually represent a conscientious attempt to ensure adequate guarantees of service. The dean of a school of engineering said:

I run the computer center only because I want my staff to have the best there is. I'd be happy to turn the whole thing over to an all-university system. The administration of this center is pure headache. But I'm going to hang on to it until I can be absolutely sure that my faculty will get as good or better service from a centralized facility.

In the area of administrative computer services, the experienced administrator intuitively perceives that whoever controls the content, origin, form, flow, and use of the institution's information system has considerable implicit or explicit power—or at least influence. Many presidents have the uneasy feeling that the nature of the reports they receive is being determined not by their needs or interests but by the imperatives of the methods of data processing. He who controls the nature and form of the reports laid on the president's desk may exert real influence on the nature and results of the president's decisions.

Pressures on the president come not only from the academic community. Some trustees, especially businessmen who have used computers in corporate research and management, express keen interest in computers and data processing. Some have asked that the president and his top staff attend special workshops. In some cases, the trustees have made special efforts to obtain funding for adequate facilities. Members of legislative committees who examine the budgets of state institutions demand information regarding efficiency of operation and are increasingly aware that data they ask for could be supplied by a computer-assisted administrative system. In one case, trustees representing industry loaned some of their own specialists to help the college design a modern system for administrative data management.

THE PRESIDENT'S ROLE

The president who remarked glumly "All I know is what the computer tells me" may actually be receiving excellent services which fully exploit the potentials of his administrative data processing system; but as long as he feels uncertain about it, he senses a loss of control. He can relieve this uncertainty in several ways: he can ask the opinions of outside observers, he can compare his services with those provided at institutions having comparable facilities, or he can try to understand enough about the capabilities of computers to satisfy himself that he is getting what he wants or needs.

In the development and allocation of computing resources, the president has a dual role. He is a present or potential *user* of these resources and hence has a justifiable interest in getting all the potential power from an automated information system. The president is also a *provider* of services to the academic community; he must be sure adequate facilities exist for the faculty and students.

It is reasonable for the president to ask at this point: "When you say that the president should know *enough* to make these judgments, how much is *enough?*" In a sense, this report is an extended answer to this question.

Knowing the Facts

During the study reported here, the investigators were not as surprised as were some of the administrators they interviewed to find out how many computers existed on their campuses. At one large state university, the computer center director, interviewed early in the day, listed five computers used by the university. By the end of the day, a total of seventeen had been counted, including some of whose existence the president's staff had not been aware! One faculty member, it turned out, used three computers 24 hours a day, paid for out of his own research grants. The quiet flowering of computer plants which has escaped the notice of the administration may be evidence of an ingenious and effective faculty, one capable of looking after its own needs and interests, but it may also reveal a failure on the part of the administration to grasp the problem it must solve— making the most effective overall use of the institution's resources.

Computing on college campuses has such a relatively short history that it is difficult to find historical guidelines. The novelty of the tool encourages experimentation but may also lead to apparent anomalies or at least to the requirement for new criteria. For example, one administrator, faced with the argument that a new and larger computer must replace the machine already in use 16 hours a day, discovered that one graduate student was responsible for more than 40 percent of the time being used. Investigation revealed that the student, a poultry science major, was making studies of chicken feed! It is easy to smile at this classic little anecdote, but others could be cited which turn out, on deeper investigation, to have more serious implications. If the chicken feed study were to lead to formulas which markedly increase the profits and productivity of the whole poultry industry, the results might more than justify the cost of the study. (The question of how these costs should be met, of course, is another story.)

Unchecked and uncoordinated proliferation suggests entrepreneurism and improvisation forced upon those who need computers and who see no feasible central plan for obtaining them. Absence of a plan means absence of criteria for effective achievement of goals. Having no plan also suggests that the administrator is not in full control of all the educational resources of the institution. He has not grasped or accepted the importance of the needs which the computer entrepreneur has tried to satisfy by himself.

Management Functions

When asked for a simple statement of the primary purpose of administration in higher education, most presidents reply along these lines: to provide and allocate the resources necessary to create an environment for effective learning and scholarship. In the context of society as a whole, it seems obvious that the development of computer resources is of concern at the very highest levels of educational leadership. Although it is rash to argue that the computer is the administrator's most important or pressing problem, it is significant that the computer seems to cast its shadow across so many problem areas in which its critical role is not immediately self-evident. The computer may not be *sufficient* to solve all administrative and academic problems, but in an increasing number of instances it is proving itself *necessary*.

The basic administrative uses of computers are either *transactional* or *managerial*. In almost every case, automated systems are employed for routine transactions—accounts and budgets, payroll, receiving and disbursing, student registration, cumulative records, grade reporting, scheduling. The existence of a large and comprehensively inclusive data base is no guarantee that the data will be used for managerial

purposes—planning, modeling, simulation, institutional research, decision-making. The existence of a sophisticated computer facility and a well-developed data base does not lead to these higher uses unless specific attention is devoted to developing them. Using a computerized model for facility planning, one college system discovered methods of scheduling which paid for the computer processing many times over. The administrator who has not exploited the full potential power of these relatively new techniques is not just failing to get the full dollar value out of the computer-based system, he is neglecting opportunities to use the computer as a tool for allocating other educationally significant resources with optimum efficiency.

In large institutions the very richness of the environment may produce complexities for management which require complex analysis and control in order to serve the whole community of faculty and students to best advantage. In smaller institutions, the comparative scarcity of resources, including funds, implies the need for equally careful allocation of resources under quite different constraints. (For example, a miscalculation of income of half a million dollars will have less impact on a large institution with an annual budget of $130 million than it would have on a small one with a $5 million program.)

LOOKING AHEAD

Trends in the form and content of higher education and the shifting roles of small and large, public and private institutions will create demands for varying kinds and levels of management information systems. The degree of control over current programs and resources and future plans may also affect the institutions and their roles. It is difficult to cite any major trend or problem in higher education—in curriculum, staff, students, facilities, costs—which will not in some degree affect and in turn be affected by the computer and its attendant systems.

Typically, few institutions are even now able to exploit all the resources of the second-generation computers of yesterday, and by the time the new generation of computers has had its full impact on higher education, yet a fourth generation, the computers of the 1970's, will be available. Compared to some other social institutions, colleges and universities have in general not been able to move as rapidly as most business and industry in using computers. Academicians shun comparisons with the latter sector of society because of the differences in motivation and value systems, but one need not share the motives of the world of commerce in order to make good use of what commerce and industry have learned about effective use of scarce resources in the face of growing complexities and burdens.

Before too much time, effort, and money are committed to solving today's problems, to say nothing of the amount even now being spent on solving yesterday's, it may be helpful to look at the implications of what little can be predicted with some safety about problems and relevant technologies of the future.

Statistical projections, assisted by common sense, show continuing growth in enrollments in higher education, both in absolute numbers and in the percentage of the eligible population seeking higher education at all levels (from lower division to graduate and professional). Costs will continue to rise as faculty and facilities increase in size and improve in quality, even if inflation were not to continue to affect costs. Rising endowments and increased state and federal support bring management problems. The rising costs of education increasingly focus the attention of both taxpayer and legislator on the efficiency of administration in public higher education, posing problems for the administrator which will require every powerful tool available for their solution.

From another quarter comes the pressure for increased effectiveness of instruction and for the development of new curricula to meet changing and growing demands of society and of new technologies. The potential roles of the computer as an aid to instruction have barely begun to be studied. The explosive growth of scientific information and of documentary collections will require new methods of management if the growing value of man's knowledge is to be exploited. Increasing demands for knowledge, compounded by rapid growth in man's knowledge, appear to be creating increasing values for information, but this value cannot be translated into utility without vastly improved means of storing, indexing, collating, browsing, searching, and retrieval—again the computer appears to provide a vital (but not single) answer. Even if the severe technological problems of information storage and retrieval are solved, the scheduling and switching problems involved in effective information traffic control will require computing devices of great speed and flexibility. Access to tomorrow's great libraries may well be by way of the computer console or its remote stations.

The apparently high cost of today's large computers seems forbidding at first glance. However, several trends operate to help reduce the cost of various kinds of administrative and academic applications. The efficiency of computers has multiplied faster than costs. In addition, methods of sharing computers among a group of users reduce the cost to each, though the problem of developing time-sharing systems makes initial costly demands for programmers and system analysts. Problems of sharing large files of information are also under study and may create some new difficulties for system designers. Many experts believe, however, that the next generation of computers, using new electronic techniques, may be so small and so inexpensive that the cost of using large computers may be reduced by making large numbers of miniature computers available to users on site, with improved accessibility.

The point is that while thought is being devoted to effective utilization of currently available computer resources, time should also be devoted to thinking ahead to the system and operating implications of the next generation. Some who plan ahead will be able to leap more readily into the jet-age stage without retracing the history of automation on each campus. Whatever happens, the administrative and academic communities can no more afford to ignore or postpone thinking about the implications of computers than they can the implications of new media of communication and the changing nature of society as it reacts to the forces of automation and the new information technology.

2

MACHINES AND CAPABILITIES

The modern electronic computer has produced a revolution in science, engineering, industry, and commerce, and has permeated our whole society. Our nationwide investment in computers has soared from $700 million in 1958 to $7 billion in 1964. Throughout this period, about four percent of these computers have been located on university and college campuses. Despite this small percentage, colleges and universities have played a key role in computer development. The first computers were conceivevd and built at universities, and campus computing centers are currently developing more advanced systems programs that will permit all computer users easier and more satisfactory access to computers.[1]

PRIOR TO WORLD WAR II, the electronic digital computer as we now know it did not exist except in the minds of scientists such as John von Neumann and Vannevar Bush. Work on such problems as the development of the atomic bomb dramatized the need for assistance in vast calculations, and, not long after, the first primitive computers appeared in a few campus laboratories. Even with the rapid development of computers, 1950 found no college equipped even with one commercial computer. By 1955, fewer than 25 had acquired some of the early equipment, and even by 1960 less than 150 campus computers could be counted. By 1966, the number had exceeded 600, and by 1970 it is estimated that more than one-half of all colleges and universities will have at least one computer. There are a few large universities with more than 20 on a single campus. Some large statewide systems have multimillion dollar inventories. No matter how explosive this growth may seem, it has been slower in higher education than in industrial, military, or government organizations.

[1] *Digital Computer Needs in Colleges and Universities* (Washington: Committee on Uses of Computers, National Academy of Sciences, 1966), p. 1.

THE CURRENT SITUATION

The impact of the computer on society, and hence on the curriculum, has been compared to that of movable type and the printing press since Gutenberg. There are important differences (speed of development and dissemination, cost, technological complexity are a few), but the important parallel lies in the common concern with the way in which information is generated, transmitted, and used. As Marshall McLuhan and others have argued, society is profoundly affected by the way in which information is handled. No one in Gutenberg's time could imagine the impact of printing—on education alone, on method, content, audience, and institutional forms. The computer has already transformed or greatly altered methods of investigation, scholarship, and teaching; it has even suggested new fields of research and new approaches to the solution of complex social problems.

There is scarcely a field of scholarship or learning in which the computer has not already been recognized as having a significant role. It is obvious that the quantitative sciences require increasing use of computers. Volumes have been written on the uses of computers in biology, sociology, anthropology, psychology, library science, linguistics, history, archaeology, political science, law, medicine, management science, education, economics, and even the fine arts. One university already offers a course in computer-generated musical composition, and exhibitions of computer-generated art and sculpture are noted with increasing frequency.

The dean of the faculty in one small state university explained why he was struggling to educate his faculty in the lore of computing:

> The computer is an important tool of thought, not just in doing hard work fast but in forcing people to state their problems clearly and think out what they want to do. It extends a man's mind and gives him new insights in his field. I tell our staff flatly that if they aren't using computers, they're not only working too hard, they're passing up opportunities to cross new frontiers of investigation. Some of our students are ahead of our faculty in their grasp of this.

Number and Size

One of the signs of the growing significance of computers in our society, and in higher education, is to be found in the figures on the growth of the number and value of computers. In 1960 there were only about 1,000 computers in the United States, with a value of about $2.5 billion. Five years later the number had increased to 35,000 and the value to $8 billion. By 1970 it is predicted that the number will increase to 75,000 with a total value of more than $18 billion.

The number of engineers, scientists, and technical personnel needed to support this industry, to keep this many computers busy, is almost impossible to estimate. It is widely suggested that by 1970 over one-half of the working population will have something to do with computers. It is estimated that nearly one-half of all students *now* engaged in four-year college programs will need to use computers in their professional work. Predictions for the next decade are even more impressive, or threatening, depending on one's viewpoint.

On the nation's college campuses the growth has followed this trend. Unfortunately no thorough census has been made recently. The Rosser report[2] is thorough but out-of-date. The annual survey of the American Association of Collegiate Registrars and Admissions Officers[3] is timely but concerned primarily with computers used in registration and admissions systems. A safe estimate would seem to be: More than 30 percent of American colleges now use computers of some kind. In recent years, 80 to 100 institutions (or about 4 percent) acquired their first computer each year. The Rosser report recommends government support adequate to allow colleges to spend $200 million in this year, and 20 percent more in each succeeding year. The number of computers installed at colleges increases at the rate of 45 percent each year. Universities that have computers tend to have more than one.

The 1965-66 AACRAO survey elicited 1,350 responses, a substantial number of them from junior colleges. Computer use was found to correlate with size of institution in the following way:

ENROLLMENT CATEGORY	PERCENTAGE USING COMPUTERS
Under 1,000	7.3%
1,000-4,999	40.5%
5,000-9,999	83.6%
Over 10,000	96.1%

In the academic community, the following general trends define the environment for future administrative thought and action:

[2] *Op. Cit.*
[3] *Electronic Data Processing Survey* (Knoxville: AACRAO, annually). See Appendix.

Computers exist at colleges of all types or are being used at other locations by many institutions which do not have their own.

The number of users on most campuses is continually increasing at an accelerating rate.

In many colleges, the computer is viewed as a resource as important—and as generally significant—as the library.

At some institutions, computer programming is a required course for all entering freshmen who have not already taken it in high school.

A trend is beginning to appear for faculty and even students (especially at the graduate level) to be attracted to a particular institution because of the quality of its computing resources.

Though it is not widely known by college administrators, there exist computing resources of a size and cost adequate to meet the minimum needs of an institution of any size and type. One administrator says, "When you hear a college say it can't afford a computer, it means they haven't yet realized they have to have it." Some of the needs of smaller colleges may at present best be met by sharing equipment and systems with other institutions.

WHAT IS A COMPUTER?

Those who are not familiar with computers sometimes tend to regard them as being merely overgrown and remarkably speedy adding machines and hence of only mechanical interest. To construct a machine to perform familiar arithmetic operations at very high speed was indeed one of the first objectives of the scientists who developed the computer. But of much greater significance is the modern computer's ability to perform a sequence of instructions, to take account of the results at key points in the process, and then *to modify its own instructions in accordance with precise logical rules laid down by its user.*

It is essential to grasp the implications of these words; otherwise one may not see beyond the obvious advantages of speed, the capacity to store large quantities of information, and accuracy of calculation. Before expanding on this point, it is necessary first to establish a few simple facts about the way in which a computer uses information.

A Storehouse for Facts

The computer memory may be thought of as a beehive with many discrete cells, each containing a *number*, and each cell itself being designated by a numerical *address* which can be used to identify its location. One can direct the computer to store a number in cell 1234 and then later modify it or fetch it from that address.

Purely numerical information, useful as it is, does have its limitations, and it is perhaps partly the common conception of the computer as simply an arithmetic device which makes it seem of such trivial intellectual interest at first glance. However, it was perceived that numerals could represent more than quantities. Using pairs or sets of numbers to represent alphabetic characters and special symbols, it is possible to store words and sentences. Numerals are also used to represent *instructions* to the computer, which may be modified, either by replacement or by arithmetic operations. For example, the numeral 71 can, in different contexts, mean the *number* 71, or the *letter* A, or the *operation* of addition.

In addition to being able to perform basic arithmetic operations, computers are capable of making logical comparisons between two facts. For example, the computer can be instructed to compare facts A and B in such ways as: Is A different from B? Is A greater (or less) than B? Is A (or B) a zero?

The answer to such questions is always a simple "yes" or "no." It then becomes possible for the user to specify what is to be done next in either case, thus establishing a series of contingent actions, similar to a set of instructions a busy president might give his secretary. "Ask Dean Smith if he can have lunch with me today. If he says 'yes,' make a reservation at the Faculty Club. If he says 'no,' ask him about the next day." This string of alternatives can be repeated until one of two things happens: either a successful engagement is scheduled or the patience of the inquirer is exhausted (which limit can be specified by the number of tries the secretary is to make, or by the last date by which the desired engagement will have any relevance because the Dean will have been fired).

The results of such logical comparisons can be used to search through a designated set of cells and find something (search until a prespecified key word is found, for example), to sort lists of numerals or words into some desired order, to match a word with a definition in a dictionary, to identify the shape of a line by matching its graphed coordinates, to find unused cells in which to store new information, to let a process continue until some criterion is satisfied, and so on.

A sequence of instructions, together with specifications of what is to be done under every foreseeable contingency (including the occurrence of an unexpected one!), is called a *program*. Any process which can be described in precise terms can be carried out or executed by the computer.

A Program Plus Speed

We need now to put the notion of "programmability" together with a more precise notion of what kinds of speeds are possible. In the most modern computers, instructions can be performed in millionths of seconds (microseconds), or even in billionths of seconds (nanoseconds). Information can be fetched from a storage cell with similar speed. For example, if a computer requires one microsecond to fetch and add two numbers, it can add a million of them in one second; if it takes one microsecond to compare a key word with an item in a storage cell, as in searching a file, it can examine words at the rate of a million per second. (Recall that the Third Edition of the Merriam-Webster *Unabridged Dictionary* boasts less than half a million major entries.)

The point of the foregoing is so obvious that it may be missed. If a complex process, involving a vast file of information and many decision points, can be performed at speeds approaching that of light, it is efficient to let the computer repeat what might, upon detailed study, seem quite crude or brute-force procedures until a desired result is obtained. The means by which a computer sorts a set of words into alphabetic order are extremely crude compared to those which would be used by a clerk with a card file, but at extremely high speeds such methods enable the computer to alphabetize a thousand words during the time it takes the human file clerk to alphabetize a dozen. Thus speed combined with the capacity to perform very simple tasks one after another according to a logical plan and with virtually unerring precision gives man a tool which vastly exceeds his own capacity to recognize, recall, organize, or otherwise manipulate conventionally useful information.

The Computer Imperative

A final point should be made here, though it is discussed at greater length later. That it is *possible* to program the computer is no less important than that it is *necessary* to do so. This requirement forces the human user to understand in great detail, and with keen logical insight, what it is he wants to do. This *computer imperative*, forced on the human user by the fact that the computer does only what it is instructed to do, is itself a powerful stimulant to the mind. The computer frees man from the drudgery associated with repetitive and mundane clerical labor, but it does not free him from the necessity to think, especially about the criteria he wishes to apply to enable the computer to trace its way at nearly the speed of light along the manifold branches of a systematic process and finally arrive at what he wants to know.

HISTORICAL ASPECTS OF COMPUTING

The situation faced today and tomorrow by the administrator has two principal antecedents: the use of punched card methods and accounting machines for the mechanization of administrative records, and the relatively sudden and increasing use of electronic digital computers since the 1950's.

Punched card processing, involving keypunches, sorters, tabulators, and the whole family now usually called EAM (electromechanical accounting machines), has been used by some institutions since the early 1920's. At first glance, the modern computer may appear to be simply a speeded-up and fancier version of elementary punched card equipment. In a sense this is true, but it overlooks a more important characteristic: computers may be programmed to perform tasks of great complexity not requiring human intervention. The compound of increased speed, complexity of programming, more readily accessible data storage, and freedom from the necessity for human intervention at key points in processing—all characteristic of computers— adds up to a resource so much more powerful than punched card equipment as to be qualitatively different.

The first modern computers were conceived and designed primarily for scientific purposes. They were needed for complex and tedious calculations in such fields as ballistics and high-energy physics; hence the earliest computers were developed for engineering and physics departments of large universities. Computers which used vacuum tubes (and required large amounts of floor space and air-conditioning equipment) are often referred to as first-generation computers. The second-generation computer featured small transistors (cheaper, cooler, and more durable than vacuum tubes). The size and expense of these machines were much reduced. Third-generation computers, now available, feature a wide variety of improvements—miniaturization, multiple channels for input and output of information, bigger and cheaper storage systems, and simplicity of operation accompanied by greater flexibility of application. Fourth-generation computers, now in laboratory stages of development, will feature increased miniaturization, even larger memories, new modes of storage, speeds limited only by the speed of light, parallel processing (simultaneous operation on several sets of data which are processed in the same way), and aids to programming which are engineered into the computer itself.

The nature of the adminstrative task, of course, determines the technology used to perform it, but it is also important to note that the nature of the tasks is also affected by the emerging processing technology. As the two streams of development (punched card equipment and computers) have merged, totally new potentials have appeared which must be understood if the administrator is to grasp the long-range significance of the computer as a tool to assist him in his work.

TECHNOLOGY AND SYSTEMS

In a *manual* system forms and procedures are usually designed to accommodate the human processors, including considerations of ease in writing on forms, alphabetizing, counting, adding, summarizing, storing, filing, and so on.

In a *punched card system* conversion from manual procedures at first simply mechanizes what was previously done. The machines themselves impose restrictions—space for only 80 or 90 characters on a punched card, 120 type positions on a tabulating machine, and limited character sets (only numerals and uppercase letters). Production schedules are limited not so much by the number of clerks and their working hours but by the fixed speeds of machine processing. The user of the punched card system gradually becomes aware that the information on cards constitutes a flexible file which can be reorganized for the production of reports not feasible under a manual system. In the preparation of budgets, for example, trial runs may be made rapidly and accurately under various assumptions. One can in effect *experiment with data* with a speed, convenience, and accuracy not feasible under a manual system.

In a *computerized* system there are usually several identifiable developmental phases or stages. In the first phase, the computer is used simply to do faster what was earlier done with punched card machines. In a system using magnetic tapes, it may even be some time before it is realized that the old rigid 80-character limitation of the card has disappeared and that data can be stored on tapes in almost any file entry size. In the second phase, advantage is taken of the full range of characteristics of the computer. More and more of the minor rule-following human tasks and quality controls are taken over by fully programmed processing internal to the computer. The speed of the computer is utilized in more complex analyses, in more frequent trial runs—the beginnings of simulation. The user can then ask questions of the form, "What would happen if we . . .?" with regard to policies, standards, and varying contingencies.

Concurrently with the gradual development of a punched card or a computerized system, there are phases of reporting style which directly impinge on the administrator and his work. In the first flush of enthusiasm for automated processing, the system operators may deluge the administrator with information. As one vice-president for finance said, "Automation may have helped the clerks, but I'm drowning in a sea of paper."

In later, more mature phases, the administrator learns more about the characteristics and possibilities of the system and demands that reports be more readily understandable, with only the summary facts he requires for decisions, planning, and control. In some circumstances, exception reporting becomes the rule as certain vigilances are built into the system. In one state university, a cost control system automatically compares expenditures with budgets for research contracts, and only those underruns or overruns exceeding certain established limits are listed.

In addition to routine reports, special reports and studies can be prepared on short notice to meet occasional or unforeseen needs of the administration. In the best systems the administrator understands enough about the data files and the response capabilities of the system to know what to ask for; hence he does not need to take time to examine matters not currently of interest. *It is in knowing what it is possible to ask for* that the administrator comes to master the system and extract full value from its potentials.

Three fairly elementary points should be considered:

1. Computers come in all shapes and sizes. Which one an organization selects depends on its own peculiar requirements.

2. Although all computers are general in purpose, some can do more things more easily than can others. Some are more naturally suited to certain classes of application (e.g., science, commerce, instruction).

3. Consequently, it is clear that selecting a computer is actually only one (important) part of the larger process of designing a system to meet its potential user's needs.

Osborn

THE COMPUTER: ITS PARTS AND FUNCTIONS

Most modern computers are composed of a constellation of several interconnected units, each performing one or more of the complex of data processing functions. Consequently, except in the case of very small self-contained machines, a wide range of options exists. The various parts of the computer come in different sizes and different speeds and can be acquired and replaced independently. They are even sometimes acquired from different manufacturers. And if it appears desirable at some time to change the capabilities of the computer center in some way, it is possible to modify, replace, or add a component to the computer. The administrator needs to understand a few of the terms he will hear in general discussions or read in reports.

The Hardware Constellation

It may be helpful to examine a schematic floor plan of a typical computer constellation, as in Figure 1.

1. The *Central Processor* may be a single machine unit, housed in a so-called main frame, or several separate units. The external control unit is often seen as a panel of lights, switches, and buttons, or a typewriter keyboard. This constellation of devices performs the essential control functions and is the heart of the network joining the various devices which constitute *the* computer.

2. The *Control* functions operate according to a computer *program*, taking each instruction in turn and calling upon the other units of the computer to perform the indicated actions—call a number out of storage, add two numbers, or print a line of results.

3. The unit labelled *Processor* performs the arithmetical and logical operations on the data. It adds and subtracts, compares numbers, and so on. It obeys one instruction at a time subject to the computer program.

4. *Storage* units hold the program and the current data that the program will act upon. The figures below give some indication of the typical relative capacity, speed, and cost of such units:

STORAGE UNIT	CAPACITY (millions of characters)	TRANSFER RATE (thousands of characters per second)	TYPICAL COST (cents per character)
Drums	2 to 66	9 to 2,000	8.0¢
Disc	15 to 234	22 to 184	0.4¢
Cartridge unit	2 to 680	38 to 156	0.04¢
Tape	2 to 50	2 to 600	0.01¢

5. *Input* units are the means by which information is entered

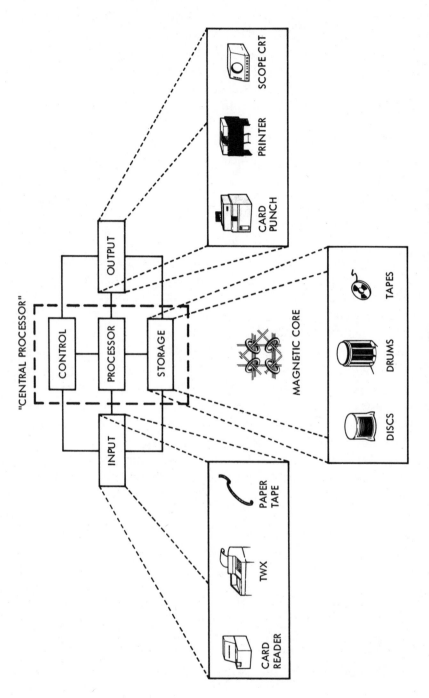

FIGURE 1: COMPONENT UNITS OF A TYPICAL COMPUTER

into the computer. These may include punched card or paper tape readers, typewriter keyboards, or other computers.

6. *Output* units provide the means for displaying or receiving the results of computer processing. These devices include typewriters, card-punching machines, printers, or other computers.

Hardware and Software

So far we have merely suggested the complexity of a computer and the number of variables which exist in designing a specific complement for an installation. Actually the situation is more complicated than even this would imply. The machine itself is still an intricate device, speaking a *language* of its own, incapable of doing any work outside of its basic list of *commands* (such as add, subtract, compare). What the computer still needs is a set of programs to make it more easily used and to do some of the more general operations. These considerations, so frequently overlooked in discussions of computer hardware, are called *software*. Precise definitions of this word vary: sometimes it is used to mean all parts of the system other than the hard, physical reality of the machine itself and sometimes it is specifically restricted to computer programs. We will use software to mean those computer programs, systems, and procedures which expand the usefulness of the computer to the user, make it possible to communicate in a language more like that of the user, and make it as easy as possible for the user to state his problems in familiar terms.

Essentially, software makes it possible, with increasing degrees of ease, for each class of user to communicate his wishes and his data to the machine and to interpret what the machine does with them. In early computers the user who wished to compute the square root of x had to specify step by step how to compute it. Today the user can simply write SQRT(X) and the computer supplies, from the software system, the necessary procedure. Most early computers used a number base other than ten (two or eight, for example), and the user had to translate familiar decimal numbers into the required form —a very tedious requirement. Modern software permits the user to enter data in almost any form, the computer taking over all the drudgery of translation. A more sophisticated example is the software procedure which permits the user to draw a line on a special metal *tablet* and have it read directly by the machine without having to describe the line in terms of Cartesian coordinates or an equation.

It should be emphasized that even computer specialists disagree about what the word *software* means. Some cut the Gordian knot with the following definition: "Software is everything other than the hardware and human beings required in the process of using computers to follow procedures specified with optimum convenience to the user."

Languages

Part of the job of programming, called *coding*, consists of converting into the language of the computer precise statements of procedures to be followed. Early in the development of computers it was realized that coding is largely a mechanical operation and hence itself subject to automation. Several languages have been developed which allow the programmer to specify procedures in a more sophisticated way; for example, compilers translate procedure statements into the machine's code. The reader should be warned, if he has never seen a program written in one of these languages (such as COBOL or FORTRAN,[4] two of the most widely used), that they are languages only in a very special sense. They are grammatically very simple; they are primarily imperative (since their function is to tell a machine what to do next) rather than descriptive; they are strictly defined so as to make ambiguity all but impossible. If one expects them to look like basic English and be comprehensible to the novice, he will be disappointed. Yet they have been a revolutionary development and have cut the cost of programming by a large factor.

Operating Systems

Suppose that a user approaches the computer with a deck of cards containing a program he has written in the FORTRAN language. He wants the FORTRAN compiler to be read into the main memory, and he wants his program compiled on tape. If there are no errors, he wants his compiled program read back into memory, and he wants it to run. If it goes haywire, writing nonsense on tapes that do not belong to him or erasing the contents of the discs, he wants it

---

[4] Acronyms for "COmmon Business Oriented Language" and "FORmula TRANSlation."

stopped, preferably *before* it happens, with a suitab'
message given to him.

Who does this for him? No one. There is a progra..
machine, called an *operating system* (or *executive*), which proviuc
such basic services. The user specifies which of the services he wants
and in what order. The operating system will find the FORTRAN
compiler (which may be on disc or tape); if it does not have the
proper tape, it will print out a message asking for it; it will save the
compiled program, let it operate, and protect the rest of the system
from programs with errors.

Such programs vary a great deal in complexity. The larger and more
expensive machines will have more complex executives, both to
provide greater service to the user and to save valuable time. It may
accept one user's requests at a time, as in the example above, or it
may take a stack of jobs, sort them into a convenient order, and do
them in the most expeditious fashion. It may even, as we shall see
below, do several of these things at once.

Finally, the software may include small programs which perform
useful common operations. This saves the individual user from writing them again and again. The most common subroutines take care
of simple mathematical functions, manipulate input and output
equipment, arrange characters in proper format for printing, and
so on.

COMPUTER TIME AND USER TIME

Earlier in discussing computer hardware, there was brief mention
of the speed of computer components and how these are related to
cost. The speed of the computer is also obviously related to the
amount of work that can be done in one day. But any description
of speed in terms of so many millions of operations per second lacks
context and is difficult to interpret meaningfully. The user cares not
whether the computer can perform 100,000 additions per second if
it takes two days to get a simple piece of work done. From the point
of view of the user, the significant parameters of time are not
measured in operations per second but in operations or tasks per day
or (frequently) per week. It is the total time it takes to process his
job. This key figure, the total elapsed time from giving the necessary
materials to the computer center until receipt of the finished work,

is commonly called *turnaround* time. The one fact about turnaround time all users agree upon is that the shorter it is the better. This point needs a little qualification. There is, on any given occasion, an optimum turnaround time for each user, beyond which speed is of no value to him. This figure will differ among users depending upon the nature of their work.

Examples of Users

In order to understand the implications of turnaround time let us consider three different computer centers and how they will serve different users. Computer Center A is so backlogged with work (most of it mysteriously labelled "highest priority") that the average user does not get his job back until three days after he sends it in. Computer Center B is able to provide turnaround time of one day. Computer Center C can usually return jobs in less than an hour. Three different users will serve as examples of individuals to be served by these centers: a member of the accounting staff who must produce certain periodic reports; a professor making statistical analyses of laboratory data; and an administrative programmer writing a procedure to assist in fall registration.

The accountant produces all of his reports on a fixed schedule and so he can learn to live with very slow turnaround time. If the report is due on Thursday, he will send his data to Computer Center A on Monday. Additional service provided by faster turnaround time is of little value to him. However, there are limits to the time he can wait. If, for example, the report which is due on Thursday is to include transactions made on Wednesday, then the situation is very different. The service provided by Computer Center A is no longer tolerable. Any service must be fast enough to fall within the reaction time tolerances set for the whole system.

The second user, a faculty member, assembles batches of data from his experiments and wants to see an analysis of them before he begins another experiment. If he must wait three days, his work is stalled for three days, and his laboratory and equipment are not used. If he gets the better service provided by Center B, he will probably be satisfied. If he gets the results within an hour, as he would from Center C, he is probably getting faster service than he needs; with the press of other work, he will not have time to study the results until the next day anyway. Center C is a luxury which he will be happy to have but which he does not really need.

The registrar's programmer wants to run sample data to find any mistakes in his programs. There will be some, as in all new programs of any complexity. At Center A, he can correct his errors only every three days. At Center B, he can do so once a day; this is better but still not good. At Center C, he can be kept busy preparing jobs, studying results, correcting errors, and making progress all day long (and he will probably meet the fall deadline).

OPTIMIZING RESOURCES

The primary administrative objective is one of optimum use of resources. If the user must wait for what he regards as too long for the results of his job, his time is being wasted—and possibly the time of other individuals and resources (such as the scientist's laboratory and equipment). But service which is faster than he can use is also wasteful of the resources of the computer center. For fast turnaround means that the center has little or no backlog of work; this may mean that there are times when the machine is idle. Much thinking has gone into this problem, from technical studies of queuing theory to systems of variable charging rates for degrees of convenience and service. The latest attempt to solve the problem of access to the computer is a new way of using computers altogether and threatens to revolutionize much of computer usage. It is called *time-sharing*.

Operating Methods

To explain this new and important concept, some historical perspective is needed. The simplest way to use a computer (and for small and inexpensive machines it is still a good way) is to let the user walk up to it, operate it himself, and then go away. If someone else is using the machine when he arrives, he waits or comes back later. This mode of operation is called *open shop* because any user can walk in, at his convenience or by appointment.

In installations that are very busy and/or very expensive, this is inefficient. The user does not operate the machine frequently enough to be very adept at it. Furthermore, since he is running his own program, he is likely to tinker with it if anything goes wrong rather than let someone else use the machine while he analyzes the trouble. Consequently most large installations hire skilled professional computer operators who have an unbiased attitude toward all of the jobs and will not try to rewrite the program at the machine. Their presence makes the center a *closed shop*.

In the simplest closed shop operation, the operator will take one job at a time, in the order in which it arrives, read the instructions, run it, and label the output for the user. But this system also has its inefficiencies. When these become intolerable, a new system may be designed, called *batch-processing*, which allows the operator to take all of the jobs that are waiting to be run, combine them into a single set of inputs, and let the machine run one directly after the other without pause. The advantage of this is clear: the machine does not stand idle while the operator reads the instructions for each individual job.

Until a few years ago, most of the largest computer installations were run in this more efficient way. But batch-processing, pure and simple, was not the best answer for everyone concerned: the larger the batches, the more efficiently can the center be run, but the longer and more inflexible the turnaround time. Further refinements were made in such systems. Some systems use the computer to help schedule itself, so that short jobs are run first and longer jobs are run later. Various types of official and unofficial priority schemes are used. More important users, or those willing to pay extra, get preferred treatment.

Multiprogramming is a technique to take advantage of the inefficiencies present in individual programs themselves. In this mode of operation, two or more different programs are resident in the computer at the same time. Under the surveillance of an operating system, one program is executed until it reaches a point at which a mechanical delay would occur—usually for some sort of input or output activity. At such times, the central processor is free for another program. This provides for overlapping several programs to achieve better utilization of the various components of the system.

TIME-SHARING EXPLAINED

Time-sharing is an extension of this technique. Portions of a relatively large number of programs (in some cases more than one hundred) are resident in the computer at one time, and the computer switches from one to another in rotation. Each program is allowed to run until a delay occurs (as in multiprocessing) or until its allotted time (which will only be on the order of fractions of a second) runs out. On a large modern machine, the rotation is fast enough and the allotted time segments are long enough to allow each program to proceed as though it were receiving continuous service from a smaller and slower computer.

One analogy which may help to explain time-sharing, as it appears to the typical user, is that of a chess match at which a master player moves from board to board around a circle of several (usually much slower and less skillful) players. The master makes his move on Board 1, moves on to Board 2, and so on around (say) ten boards. By the time the slower player on Board 1 has figured out what he wants to do next, the master has moved around the circle and back to Board 1, ready to respond again. Similarly in a multiprocessing or time-sharing system which may use a card reader operating at 600 cards a minute, the computer may use the (relatively long) interval between the reading of one card and another to do quite a bit of work on another job for which the data and program have already been stored. If the cards are read at the rate of ten per second, there is a split second interval between cards during which some computers can carry out as many as 100,000 operations on other programs.

The cost of such systems is enormous—not only for the additional hardware needed, but also for the incredibly complex software required to keep track of the many programs in simultaneous use. The compensating economy is that of multiprogramming, insuring optimum use of the components of the system; the central processor need not wait for input, or output devices wait for the processor. The complex of simultaneous uses presents a more balanced set of demands on the hardware system than any single program can. But this economy would not outweigh the costs, and the concept would have aroused scant interest, were it not for another idea which complements it: *on-line operation.*

Since the program is not tying up the entire computer when it is waiting for input or slowly doling out its output, one character at a time, it once again becomes economical to use relatively slow and cheap input/output devices such as typewriters. Since many programs are operating simultaneously, many of these devices can be in use at the same time. Time-sharing allows many users to interact with the

computer simultaneously, each feeling as though he were using the computer alone. Although each user exploits only a fraction of the speed of the machine, this fraction far exceeds his ability to interact or notice. It further allows him, for the mere cost of telephone lines, to move his input/output terminal wherever he chooses—into his office or laboratory.

At this point it is necessary to digress slightly to explain the term *buffering* as it is used in the world of computers. The administrator will sometimes hear, especially in discussions comparing costs and capabilities of hardware, that such-and-such a machine is (or is not) buffered (or "fully" buffered). Lest the administrator feel buffered from the discussion, he should be reassured that the concept is simple and often quite important in achieving high productivity on sophisticated equipment. Buffering is a hardware characteristic which exists on most large, modern computers, but it is sometimes optional. Essentially, a buffered machine provides intermediate storage for input or output; after there is a large enough group or string of inputs, the computer can gulp or spit it out all at once. Buffering performs the same function as that performed by a tray which one fills with dishes and takes all at once to the dining table instead of going back and forth to carry each individual item. While a computer's buffer is being loaded with a segment of data, it can do other useful work; as soon as the buffer is full, its contents are dumped into (or out of) the central processor. Time-sharing makes extensive use of buffering, and equipment suitable for time-sharing must feature the proper buffering components, whose existence may not be taken for granted on all computers, especially old ones or small ones.

What is the typical situation in a time-sharing system? The user has a typewriter-like machine (which costs about $100 a month plus telephone line charges and a small share of the rental of the master computer) in his office, linked directly to the computer. He types in his input, and the computer types back the output. He has the same feeling of immediate contact with the machine that the user has in a small open shop. Turnaround time, on the order of minutes, is a function of the speed of the program, the amount of output the computer must print on the relatively slow typewriter, and the ability of the user to type his input quickly without error. Since he is sharing the computer with many other users, service is surprisingly cheap. In many applications, an hour spent at a keyboard interacting with the computer will actually use only a few seconds of the central processor's time; while the user is slowly typing his inputs, the computer does not stand idle, it picks each character or line as the typewriter keys are pressed and then goes on to some other task until another signal is received. Similarly it will send its outputs at a speed acceptable to the typewriter and process other requests for service between each relatively slow character stroke.

As must be apparent even from this brief and superficial description, time-sharing is only feasible on a moderately large computing system. Very large memories are required to hold all of the programs and data for the many simultaneous users; special devices are needed for the central processor (to prevent programs from interfering with one another, for example); clocks and timing devices are required to interrupt programs whose allotted time has elapsed. Because of the complex effect time-sharing has on machine utilization efficiency and on turnaround time, its overall economy has been much debated but never clearly and unambiguously established.

Like so much in the area of computers and automation, new techniques so alter the way people actually do their jobs that there is no solid frame of reference by which to evaluate the new techniques. The computer user who begins to experiment with a time-shared system soon finds that he is doing different things with the computer and using it as a different sort of tool than he did previously.

Thinking back to the earlier examples of three typical users, it should be clear that the user who can profit from very short turnaround times (such as the registrar's programmer) will find a time-shared system very valuable indeed. The man preparing his reports on a fixed schedule will find it less valuable. However, to reject time-shared systems for him and his problem may be shortsighted, for the concept of the periodic report was devised in the context of what was possible with batch-processing computer systems. With a time-shared system, perhaps it would be wise to go back and rethink the need and schedule for this information. If the information which he had been formatting in his reports is always instantly available in the memory of the computer, perhaps his reports are no longer needed. His reports used to go to the senior administrators of the college to refer to in case they needed information. Why should they not now ask the computer directly, *when they need the data*, rather than using the machine to print all the information which they *might* need? This might well be a more effective use of the computer, the clerk, and the administrator.

Finally, consider again the scientist who wants only to analyze his laboratory data. He too may find creative ways of using time-sharing. What sorts of instruments produce the data which he wishes to analyze? Could they transmit the data directly to the computer, where they will be available whenever the scientist is ready to examine them? The computer on the other end of the campus may thus become for the experimenter an extension of his own laboratory. New devices not only solve old problems more efficiently but also may suggest redefinitions of problems and their solutions.

3

ADMINISTRATIVE SYSTEMS

THE INTRODUCTION AND GROWTH of automated data processing systems ultimately affects all levels of an organization, but the effects usually are felt at lower levels first and gradually spread upward through the ranks. Mechanized systems are just as likely to congeal as manual ones. Redesign to integrate a system more effectively or to increase its usefulness at higher administrative levels may be more difficult and expensive as the system grows in size and complexity. It is therefore worthwhile for the president to take the time, early in the day, to think ahead to what he ultimately wants and is feasible. The necessity to experiment, improvise, and revise may never be avoided entirely, but certainly it is possible to learn from the previous experiences and agonies of other institutions.

The functions of an automated administrative system may be grouped under three headings: *transactions, control,* and *planning.*

Transactional purposes are served by systems which facilitate repetitive functions associated with the various interfaces between the system and its users when information is involved. Examples are processing an application for admission, registering a student in a course, scoring a test, reporting and recording a semester mark, preparing a bill for student fees, preparing a paycheck, paying a telephone bill, purchasing a book, preparing a mailing label for the alumni magazine, making a copy of a student's record for another institution.

Transactions establish and exploit the *data base* of the system. The system's design establishes modes of input, storage, processing, and output and procedures for their control. The designer of the forms used to collect information from a student, a faculty member, or a vendor determines what information will be available in the data base. It is easy to overlook the long-range needs of other ultimate users in satisfying the immediate transactional demands of any one designer of input forms. If the admissions officer designs a student information form which gathers only what he needs to evaluate the application without considering the later needs of the registrar, the health services center, the student association, or the office of institutional research, the resulting data base may not satisfy the needs of those other users, and hence data must be gathered from additional forms and input procedures later.

Control purposes require that procedures be established to ensure that the administrative system is operating as desired or required. Means must be provided for auditing, load balancing, program evaluation, correction of overruns or underruns, supervision of personnel, maintenance of facilities, and so on. It is these purposes which are of greatest interest to the higher-level administrator. The effectiveness of such controls depends heavily on the nature of the data-base from which reports are prepared for him, and hence the design of the automated system should satisfy his needs as well as of those responsible for operations at a transactional level.

It is very often the case that in the design of an automated system the administrator will state his requirements in the context of the manual system he has last used. It is one of the responsibilities of the system designer to ensure that the administrator understands the new and improved resources the new system will make available; the demands of the administrator for information are to some extent affected by what currently is technically feasible.

It is in the satisfaction of *planning purposes* that the automated administrative system provides some of its highest payoffs. Improved forecasting is an almost elementary benefit. With the aid of the computer it is possible to use techniques of simulation and modeling for the improvement of program design. Institutional research can exploit the transactional data base for the purpose of exploring alternative ways of solving problems.

Perhaps the most important concept for the college president to understand about the implications of an automated system is that introduction of a system which provides more, better, and new kinds of information more rapidly, and especially on shorter notice, is bound eventually to affect the entire administrative system—its organization, the functions of personnel, even its objectives. *The system being optimized is not simply data processing; it is the organization as a whole.* Since the data processing personnel are not always able to see these implications, it is vitally important that the process of system design be of continuing concern at the highest levels of administration.

It is not an exaggeration to say that the "nervous system" of the administrative body is determined and defined by the nature of its information system. Increasing the speeds and reducing the drudgeries of transactional (e.g., clerical) operations is of relatively minor importance compared to the significance to the top administrator of the improved accessibility and quality of the data base upon which he can draw for purposes of control and planning. The administrators who wish to exploit fully these values and potentials must therefore know what it is possible to do. Some of this they can learn by examing what others have done elsewhere in comparable situations. For example, in the area of business management it is possible with computers to produce exception reports on a much more frequent basis than in a manual system. If expenditures for a project or budget category are markedly over or under set limits, reports can be prepared which permit the administrator to exercise short-term controls rather than having to wait for a monthly report of past history. Under such exception reporting systems with their automatic danger signals, there is a sharp reduction both in the amount of paper the administrator has to wade through to find matters requiring his attention and in the time lag between discovery and correction. Systems can also be designed to provide early warnings of difficulties in student course work which call for timely counseling or individual attention.

The use of *simulation* as an administrative technique is of growing importance. With the help of a computer program which uses the existing data base, as well as estimates of the varying probabilities with which important events could happen, combined with varying estimates of resources, enrollments, costs, and the like, the administrator can study the probable effects of various policies or criteria before committing himself to a decision regarding a program. Simulation techniques enable the administrator to estimate the effect of permitting an increase in enrollment of another 300 students, for example, or of raising tuition by another $100. The complexity of the interaction of various forces and events in such cases is so great that only with the aid of a computer can they be worked out in sufficient detail.

The experience of one university provides a good example of the potential value of simulation. A gift of $2 million was offered by an alumnus for the construction of a new dormitory which would permit an increase in residential enrollment. Without an adequate technique for estimating the cost implications of this expansion, the administration was unable to forecast the impact on the budget of the corresponding increases in faculty, library, laboratories, health services, parking, maintenance. Provided with an adequate model of the whole university system, it would have been possible to see what it would cost to accept the donor's generosity.

INFORMATION AND ADMINISTRATION

Growing institutions obviously generate more and more information, not only about increasing numbers of students and staff, but also about the problems of growth itself—facilities, library books, faculty recruitment, sources of revenue. In a manual system of administration every increase in enrollment of a hundred students may require another clerk. In an automated system such growth can often be accommodated simply by running the machines a few minutes longer.

Even in a static institution demands for information continue to increase. Each new federal program of financial aid requires the reporting of new data. Rising costs generate increased demands for information by regents, trustees, and legislators to justify rising budgets. Development and fund-raising programs need solid information to support appeals to alumni, foundations, and other sources. The chairman of one board of trustees reported a sad experience with his state legislature:

We went to them with a biennial budget 15 percent higher than the previous one. We lost every bit of the increase, because we couldn't answer some of the simplest questions of the legislative committee on finance. They cut us to pieces. Next time we've got to be ready for them.

To complicate the difficulties, costs of clerical and administrative personnel have risen to meet competition from industry and government. More clerical employees mean more floor space, desks, typewriters, and indirect costs. The comptroller of one large university reported that, although his budget had doubled in a five-year period of growth, he had reduced the clerical staff by 50 percent and *reduced* the total cost of administration by developing a computerized data system.

Rapidly changing demands for new specialties, for meeting the changing interests of students, and for research require the administrator to monitor the curriculum, the student body, the research program, and all the complex operating units of his institution on a current basis. Trends in student demand for courses and curricula must be forecast to anticipate demand for faculty and facilities. Large multi-institutional organizations, with many branches and locations, must be able to allocate resources among the members, direct the flow of student applicants to appropriate branches, and coordinate planning and development programs to maintain coherence and the advantages of shared richness of resources without imposing undue demands for conformity and without suffering too many of the constrictions imposed by size and complexity. The computerized administrative system may not provide the answer to all of these problems, but it can free the professional administrator so he can spend more time thinking and less time on paperwork. It can provide him with the information he needs to make decisions and settle arguments.

Most American colleges and universities have lagged behind government and industry in using computers for administration. Reasons for this vary, but the cited justifications generally boil down to two hard-core reasons:

A refusal to face the problem;
A refusal to pay for its solution.

"Waiting for Dr. X to retire" is the usual symptom of the first case. Dr. X is always an important member of the power structure whom his colleagues fear they may offend. He may be the comptroller, a dean, or the president. Effective administrative techniques must wait until an inoffensive way can be found to introduce them. This generally means death or retirement, rarely reeducation.

Many institutions not using modern techniques of administration are hamstrung because they cannot hire the competence to solve their problems. Translated, this means that the people who are convinced they need help may not hold the purse strings. If the administration finds money for a system analyst, only to have it diverted to hire a new associate professor of chemistry, there is little communication between the administrator interested in efficiency and the faction controlling the money.

The refusal to pay for the solution may take other than fiscal forms. The refusal of top administration to take an interest, the refusal of administrators to keep up with new techniques—these are refusals to devote time to the problem or to even respect its importance. Among the most difficult barriers to overcome is an unsuccessful experience. A blunder in their first contact with data processing may turn the influential members of the college against computing—or at any rate frighten them from trying again. Their more conservative colleagues are sometimes only too glad to accept this result. One small college tried using a computer for class scheduling. Lacking previous experience, and unaware that well-designed systems were already available locally, they plunged in prematurely; the first week of school was a madhouse, delaying the opening of classes by several days. Badly burned, the administration resolved to have nothing more to do with computers.

TRANSACTIONAL APPLICATIONS

A generalization will serve to introduce the discussion. Though there may somewhere be a model system, complete and thoroughly integrated in all aspects and departments, the survey which forms the basis for this report did not uncover it. It is not likely that one could think of a use or an application which has not been tried by someone somewhere. It is safe to say that *all* the full potentials of integrated automatic information systems have not been realized anywhere. Some areas of application (finance, for example) are most thoroughly developed in colleges where others (alumni records, for instance) have not been touched. The following discussion reports the best practices in selected institutions.

Student Records

Student records present the biggest challenge to a total system concept of operations. . . . This is the area in which we have the most overlapping of data between the file kept by one office and that of another.[1]

Part of this duplication may be unavoidable, but many of the users of student information feel that automatic data processing coupled with some centralization is the only answer to the growing volume and complexity of reports kept and the growing expense of record keeping. Paradoxically, many feel that the use of computers for student records means the risk of depersonalization. Others feel that automated record keeping is the only way to avoid increasing depersonalization. In keeping records better an automated system may serve the student more often and more individually than an antiquated and overburdened manual system. One administrator said:

Automation of records, far from burying the students in a file of numbers, gives them their only chance at individual attention in large institutions. With an automated system, one can be sure that every student comes up for surveillance every time a file.is processed. In a manual system, he's hopelessly buried in files too difficult to get at unless he's in trouble or asks a question.

Student records include data from many administrative departments and service agencies. Central billing for all student fees involves coordination with the library, the health center, the student union, the office of loans and scholarships, the campus police, the athletic departments, and sometimes local banks. One college makes it a practice to report annually to parents all fees and charges paid by students, for tax and other purposes.

Whether or not each department concerned with student records keeps its own files, and whether or not any portion of these files is automated, it is certainly desirable, and quite feasible, to regard all records as potentially parts of a single file. There is certainly no sense in having a different file numbering system for the same students, or faculty, or in having to duplicate the entry of basic data into the system. In an ideal system it should never be necessary to enter the same basic data more than once. For example, in some systems, the student is provided with a plastic card, mechanically generated from the basic file, containing his name, file number, and other essential data, and this card with his number may be used for library trans-

[1] Jack R. Woolf in *Proceedings of the Ninth College and University Machine Records Conference* (Palo Alto, Calif.: Educational Systems Corp., 1964), p. 11.

actions, health services, admission to student body events, identification, and the like.

Preprinting a form which a student is to complete, using data from his file (sometimes called a "turnaround" document), is not always feasible. But certainly the student should not be required to fill out basic data about himself time and time again. Student use of file numbers may not only reduce the amount of repetitive inputs to the system but also actually facilitate accurate identification in case of similar names, nicknames, poor handwriting.

Four years of college can generate a sizable amount of information about the student, including mental and physical health, social activities, youthful indiscretions, family problems, financial problems, and even opinions and current interests. Attention should be paid to ensuring that harmful or even embarrassing bits of information, limited to those considered essential for the record, cannot be disclosed except to persons or agencies with legitimate interests and unquestioned integrity of purpose. More than personal security is involved. The sheer bulk of such records may be unmanageable. Part of the student record system specifications and procedures should include the automatic expunging, or removal to inactive storage, of information for which no use can be seen.

Admissions

Admissions procedures supply the basic information for the student's entry into the system. At this time, information can be collected which is required to evaluate the student's potential according to the criteria for general admission. Information is gathered which can be used to counsel the student about fields of study. Institutions with branches can ask the student which location he prefers. At one institution a differential admissions procedure is used; the student may be admitted for some majors or locations but not for others. If the student is applying for an institutional scholarship, his application for this, or loans or student employment, may be part of the admissions application. Many institutions require that the student supply a social security number which is thereafter always used to collate his records from various sources and among files; others use name and date of birth. Proof of residence information may be supplied and recorded.

Data from documents submitted by the student are keypunched into cards for processing. An application fee may involve coordination with the accounting office, including provision for automatic establishment of a central fee and billing account for the student once he has been admitted or enrolled. The basic facts about the applicant may include entrance examination scores supplied by the College Entrance Examination Board or the American College Testing Program, and a parent's confidential statement for evaluation of a scholarship application.

The facts are then automatically summarized with an analysis based on rules defined by the admissions officer. This analysis provides data such as:

High school grade-point average, adjusted up or down according to the college's previous experience with applicants from the high school of origin.

Predicted grade-point averages, for the college as a whole or differentially by major or branch location, or, alternatively, probabilities associated with fixed grade-point levels (60 percent chance of obtaining a C average, 38 percent of obtaining a B, etc.).

Rank in class, transformed to a proportion (31st out of 360).

Number of high school student activities and offices held.

Notes on "subjective" factors: son of an alumnus, athletic scholarship offered, physical handicaps, military service.

Information such as this is presented in condensed and easily readable form with as many semi-automatic flags as desired. For example, if all students with a predicted grade-point average of B+ or better are automatically admissible, the applicant's inclusion in this category may be flagged by an asterisk in a special box or by presorting the report forms into groups.

A copy of this form may be prepared for use by applicant counselors who are assigned to talk with students and their parents during the spring and summer months when visits may be made to the campus. If admissions officers travel to talk with applicants, they take these forms for use in the interviews.

Once action has been taken on an applicant, one copy of the summary form is used to generate appropriate correspondence and the other is returned, suitably coded, to the computer center. Admitted applicants may be billed in advance, the necessary statements being prepared by the computer and automatically addressed for mailing in a window envelope.

As soon as the admissions process has been completed, the student's basic records are transferred to the registrar's control, though they remain in the computer center's files, with copies of extracts on the file to the accounting office (generating a permanent student account), to health services, to the appropriate deans, to the counseling center, the student activities organization, fraternities, campus religious organizations, the residence office.

Registration

The registrar, from this point on, becomes the primary user of the student's academic record. Though there may be separate files for various departments, all users will follow the same basic system and will, within limits dictated by considerations of preventing unauthorized access to sensitive data, share access to the file. The student will have the same "file number" (semantically preferable to "student number"), his name will always be spelled the same way, forms to be filled out by the student will always be preprinted from the file for continuing verification, and changes in status of any portion of the file will be shared with all users.

Registration procedures, for the first year and thereafter, will exploit the data already in the file. Instead of having to fill out forms and repeat his name, address, parents' names, birthdate, and so on, the student will receive cards or forms with as much preprinted data as possible, with the understanding that any data no longer correct (residence, for example) will be altered for updating and correcting the file.

Scheduling

Class scheduling and assignment of students to sections can be facilitated with computer processing. Several institutions have developed fast and efficient programs and procedures. These range in completeness from developing a description of class rolls after instruction begins to complete development of a master schedule and automatic assignment to sections according to predefined rules.

One purely "descriptive" post-enrollment procedure which is widely used provides the student, at the time of registration, with an envelope containing a name card imprinted with the permanent file number, local residence or dormitory address, class (presumed year of graduation), and other status data which the student is asked to verify if changes are in order, he writes only corrections; a class schedule with the place and time of meeting of all sections; and a fee schedule, preprinted on a punched card with the student's file number, to be attached to his payment.

Each instructor is given a prepunched deck of cards containing his name, room number, course number, etc., with enough cards for the maximum number of enrollees. As each student enrolls in a section, the instructor gives him a copy of the section card. To file his study list, the student simply turns in his name card together with the section cards he has been given by the instructors. His name is then mechanically picked up from his master name card and duplicated throughout all the section cards. The section cards are then sorted so that section enrollment lists can be printed for each instructor to form the basis for his records. The file of cards so generated provides the basic means for later grade reporting since it constitutes a mechanized description of enrollments by course and section. Changes in program are accomplished similarly. The student initiates a program change by asking the counselor or dean's office for a card punched with his name and file number. To change sections he picks up a section card from both the section to be dropped and the new one. He checks "drop" on one, "add" on the other, and returns the cards to the registrar. Automatic file maintenance procedures update the section enrollment file. Periodically (typically just after the final date for course changes) new section lists are printed for all instructors.

Under a second system, a master schedule is developed manually for all courses and sections. Each student files a study list. He indicates the courses he selects by checking a form or writing in the course number. These forms are keypunched, and a computer program assigns students to sections, if possible balancing loads and preserving maximum and minimum enrollments. In some programs, students who fail to meet requirements or whose schedules are unfeasible because of conflicts in time or limited section enrollments are automatically notified to see a counselor or scheduling officer to adjust their course requests.

Under a third and more highly automated system, the computer actually generates the master schedule. Four kinds of data are used: the names and time-schedule requirements of all courses, the names of faculty members teaching these courses, the characteristics and capacities of rooms associated with the courses, and the course or study list requests of students. The computer then tries to create a schedule which will permit all students to get into the courses they request, which balances the assignments and loads of faculty, and which even takes into account certain limited kinds of preference for times, places, or persons. This procedure may seem mechanical and rigid, leaving little chance for personal choice, but it was developed to meet very difficult resource constraints. However, there is no limit to the amount of human choice which *can* be programmed, providing those concerned with these choices are able to specify the rules they will apply. Only the complexity of the computer program required limits the user in choosing criteria he wishes the computer to apply in solving the problem.

The high speeds with which computers can process or even analytically generate schedules make it possible for the administrator to *simulate* the fulfillment of a schedule, under varying assumptions, and keep trying different solutions until the best one is found. The potential power of the computer to experiment with data prior to decision-making can be of great educational value. So many colleges and computer centers are working on the problems of resource allocation (of which scheduling is probably the best known) that it seems safe to say that within another decade computer programs will be commonly available which will permit an institution to offer students and faculty a wide range of personal choice and still optimize the utilization of facilities and staff time. This will tend to reduce the number of conflicts which now often limit student choices to rigidly inflexible, traditionally determined patterns.

Counseling

Counseling often begins as part of the admissions process. It may involve counseling with students during the process of devising study lists during registration. An automated system can easily provide the counselor with information such as an abstract of relevant portions of the student's file, including previous or current grades, test data, health information, student finances and employment, the status of loans, and other information needed to help students make good decisions. In some colleges the processing of grade reports automatically produces warning notices, which may be established for any level of expectancy determined by the student's own choice or by tests or other predictive data.

Grade Reporting

One system provides the instructor with a preprinted list upon which he either writes or checks term or semester grades. These lists are returned and punched, and a grade report is produced for each student. These reports can be printed on adhesive paper for updating manual files.

In all student record systems which involve student or faculty handling of cards, the greatest source of difficulty is usually not the student, whose record is at stake, but the faculty. It is surprising how difficult it is to induce many instructors to follow precise directions about methods of handling machine-readable forms. For this reason, at least until a generation of faculty emerges which takes more kindly to automation, the primary criterion for faculty-involving procedures is ease of handling.

The grade reporting system can yield, at very little cost, a most interesting by-product: studies of grade distribution by department, major, course, for example. In one study it was found that 40 percent of the grades given by one department were A's, while in another only 3 percent of students received A's. There may be good reasons for variations in practices in grading, but at least it has usually been interesting, if not startling, to see where the variations exist. Most administrators who have asked for such studies have found them extremely valuable. Another interesting study involves the comparison of student grades, by department or major, with the ability ranges of the student body, as measured by the College Board or other test scores or by high school grade-point average.

Post-Graduation Services

Alumni records and the provision of transcript services to former students represent the end of the line for student records. As students graduate relevant extracts from their files are automatically added to the alumni file. At one university, alumni contributions are solicited by frequent mailings, addressed automatically from a magnetic-tape file, and alumni are encouraged to subscribe to small regular contributions of as little as a few dollars a month if they cannot afford major contributions. Reminder notices are automatically generated for overdue installments, thank-you notes and tax receipts are prepared automatically for mailing. As the alumni director put it, "This one little application has paid for itself several times over." Again attention to individuals is facilitated rather than hampered by automation. At another college, sensitive to the "impersonal" argument, thank-you notes are hand typed but from machine-generated lists.

The Office of Institutional Research also has an interest in student and alumni records in making long-range studies of the character of the student body and the nature of the educational program. The alumni records can be used to address follow-up questionnaires. The alumni are often interested in seeing the results of such studies. One college president reported that part of the success of his fund appeals was traceable to the excellent data provided by the computerized administrative system which enabled him to make accurate predictions and to report the nature of problems with sound factual support. As another president put it, "The secret of fund raising is to tell the truth and keep your promises—and have the facts straight when you make predictions."

Staff Personnel Records

At one time personnel records could be neatly divided into *faculty* and *nonfaculty*, the latter including all nonteaching personnel. In many small colleges this is still sufficient, but larger or more specialized institutions face a somewhat more complicated picture. There are new "paraprofessional" personnel—computer programmers, highly skilled laboratory technicians, editors for college presses, and a whole range of specialized research technicians. In addition, at some large institutions more than one-half of those who do some teaching are part time—graduate students or specialists from industry and government. Often the administrator needs more than payroll records (the most elementary and usually the first staff records to develop) to assess needs for recruitment, find specialized counsel for planning and evaluation, or respond to the needs of the local community for technical advice and assistance. A *faculty record* system may include for each professional person such data as:

Identification: name, social security number, birthdate, citizenship.

Status: title, term of appointment, salary, presumed retirement date.

Assignment: department, committee memberships, office number, current teaching load, student activity assignments.

Activities: professional societies, offices held, external contracts for research, community services.

Academic record: degrees and dates, fields of study, languages, related teaching specialities.

Employment record: for each previous relevant position, title, institution, dates.

Publications: books, monographs, periodicals, musical compositions, works of art, exhibitions, performances, tours.

Inventions: patents held or pending, nonpatented contributions.

Miscellaneous data: marital status, number and ages of children, residence, special interests, military reserve and/or service record, draft status, retirement plan election.

Such records, for both full- and part-time personnel, facilitate staff searches for special assignments, committee studies, or consulting (external or internal). When appointments are being made, the names of all staff acquainted with the particular field of interest may be found to obtain their assistance or suggestions. When promotions or salary increases are being considered, relevant portions of each candidate's record may be quickly assembled. (Procedures for keeping such records up to date may be designed so as to motivate all staff members to cooperate by emphasizing the value of the file to them.)

Similar records, usually of a simpler sort, may be kept for non-faculty staff. Such files may be divided into clerical and professional if a substantial number of the latter is employed.

In addition to regular and occasional use of such files for administrative, planning, and institutional research purposes, there are some useful even if apparently trivial by-products. A printed directory of staff (name, address, home phone, extension, department) can be listed directly on multigraph masters or in other ways to facilitate printing. Announcements (notices of meetings, schedules) can be addressed quickly and selectively to designated categories of staff, or to everyone.

As in the case of student records, not all portions of the complete file of data about any one person need be maintained by a central records center. Some of the data may be under the control of the personnel department, some in the payroll office, some in the offices of the academic deans, the contracts office, and so on. However, principles similar to those used in designing student records should be observed:

Common codes and format conventions should be used so that any portion of the file, whatever its location or regular use, may be collated for research, review, or assignment searches.

Whenever possible, inputs to the files should be made only once and thereafter be made available to all qualified users.

Means must be found to protect the security of sensitive data.

Whenever possible, reports to be filled out by the staff should be preprinted with data already available, to save the time of professionals in repeated entry of old data as well as to provide an opportunity for correction and updating.

In large or even moderately large institutions, especially considering the turnover of academic administrators, it is usually impossible for the president or the faculty dean to know every instructor or to know a great deal about those known by name or sight. A computerized faculty record system can satisfy needs such as those revealed by the comments of administrators interviewed:

Suppose you're setting up a committee to consider establishing a new program. You've been talking to Professor X, who advises you to invite A, B, and C. You begin to wonder if there is someone whom you don't know who should be there. If your friend Professor Z is out of town—and he usually is—he can't tell you that the man who really knows that field is F, of whom neither you nor X ever heard. This is a big place.

After six years, an assistant professor here comes up for promotion automatically. If he doesn't make it, he's asked to move on. I'd like to be able to comb the files and find out who's coming up next year—every one of them, their salaries, and so on—so that I can estimate what it's going to save or cost me to replace them and so I can get some idea of which departments have what needs.

Sometimes committees come up with protests about teaching load versus research load and ask for more money. One department head came to me and said he had to have more instructors. I asked him how many he had now, and he couldn't tell me! This interested me, and so I began to cross-examine him. He couldn't tell me how many of his majors were graduating next June—or even last year. He couldn't tell me how many teaching hours the department had or what the average loads were. I sent him back to the drafting board. It wasn't entirely his fault. With a better record system, I wouldn't have had to ask him, or I could have verified answers if he did know them. Or he himself could have used the files to back up his case.

Trends in student majors change all the time. Classics are dying and we have 15 percent more math majors each year than the year before. I have to have a better feel for what our faculty spectrum is like, or ought to be a year from now. What little data we have of this kind is buried in manila folders in each department chairman's desk.

In faculty records, as in other administrative files, automated systems satisfy the several functions described above as transactions, control, and planning. The automated system provides a more convenient way of managing information that must be kept in order to satisfy the requirements for reports, salary, etc. It further provides the administration with a method of understanding and controlling the composition of the faculty.

This chapter has summarized some of the important and useful applications which have been developed for the automation of human records—students, faculty, and staff. Much that has been said about the general principles of automated systems is equally applicable to another important domain of administration—finance, business, and the allocation and management of resources. The general principles underlying these are treated in detail in the forthcoming revision of *College and University Business Administration* to be published by the American Council on Education in Fall 1967. The automation of such systems is the subject of the next chapter.

4

FINANCE AND BUSINESS MANAGEMENT

FINANCIAL ACCOUNTING and business management systems may be the first applications of automated data processing systems to develop in college and university administration. Those responsible for these functions are more likely to have had previous experience with computerized systems, and the parallels between the accounting problems of colleges and those of government and industry are more obvious. In some respects, the financial and business problems of institutions of higher education are more complicated than those of many commercial and industrial organizations. The budgeting and management of funds from a great variety of sources, disbursement to a wide variety of agencies and personnel, and responsibility for the management of resources and for a wide variety of quasi-business enterprises, all combine to put great pressure on the administration for wise and effective planning and control. The advantages of computerized systems, even in small colleges, are more widely accepted and more easily demonstrated in this field of application than in any other.

Though there are several ways of classifying the various functions performed because of differences in viewpoint, history, legal requirements, or scope of operations, the following examples of major areas of concern have received attention in almost every institution interested in automated systems:

Budget preparation and control: current operations, research contracts, long-range development and planning.

Disbursements: accounts payable, payroll, travel, scholarships and loans.

Revenues: accounts receivable, fee collections, gifts, rents, royalties, state and federal grants, cash deposits.

Endowment management: cash deposits, investments, securities, real estate.

Purchasing and inventory: facilities, equipment, supplies, materials.
Auxiliary activities: contracts, special laboratories, presses and publications, athletic events, book and supply stores, dormitories, cafeterias, apartment houses, industrial park development.

A comprehensive financial accounting system permits complete integration of all files and procedures across departments, programs, and functions. It provides for daily processing of transactions as well as exception reporting and close control of all revenues and disbursements—and a sound basis for budget planning. A computerized system can provide various methods for analysis and control which are not feasible under a manual system. As one comptroller explained:

The real structure of accounting is multidimensional, but most printed reports are only two-dimensional. The accountant has to decide how to present his figures to make them most meaningful to the administration. Each officer has his own kind of need. We envision a three-dimensional system—source of income, department, expenditure account—which we can slice across any pair of axes, creating a two-dimensional report. We could add other dimensions—year, for example, or a program involving more than one department or source of income.

Some colleges have transactional systems which process as many as 30,000 items a month under almost 3,000 different account headings. At one installation the volume of operations may be suggested by the fact that 8.5 million cards a year are punched. There are some institutional budgets of over $100 million a year; at one of these the comptroller said:

We produce a complete, consolidated financial report two weeks after the close of the fiscal year. In fact, we could produce status reports of the same type any time during the year on short notice. The facts available to me and to the president are never more than a week out of date.

INTEGRATED ACCOUNTS

Any one phase of financial accounting may be automated all by itself with a self-contained system for inputs, processing, checking against control criteria, record maintenance, and outputs. However, in the best systems observed an attempt is made to maximize the utility of all files and procedures for all branches of the institution. In one system for example, students receive a single monthly statement listing all payments due for a variety of purposes (tuition installment, library fines, loan installment, hospital service fees, etc.)

with payments already credited (from the previous month, from loan or scholarship reserve accounts, from student employment). How does the library fit into this example? The registrar provides the library with a complete punched card file for all students. If a student incurs a fine, his card is withdrawn from this file and reason (overdue, loss, damage) and amount are marked on it. The card is sent to the data processing center, where the facts are entered into the centralized student billing system. When the student settles his account, the amount due the library is automatically credited to the library's account.

Purchasing and inventory control may be advantageously integrated. One department may order a special device (a tape recorder perhaps), while in another department one already exists which is not being fully used. Centralized purchasing of supplies needed by different departments requires a central inventory and stock control system to ensure that the amount invested in supplies is at a minimum while the lag between order and supply is also minimized. The potential values of *systems contracting* need to be explored. Under such a system the college concludes a contract with a supplier of a commonly used item (chalk, typewriter ribbons, stationery) which is then no longer stocked by central stores. As each department orders, within its budget, the supplier ships directly to the department, which then certifies that the account is payable. The contract provides all the benefits of mass purchase discounts without the necessity to stock the item locally.

As another example of coordination, one small college maintains central records for the development office. They keep gift records and send automatic reminders and receipts. The semi-monthly gift report, shared by the comptroller, the alumni office, and the development office, orders gifts into major groups (alumni, bequests, parents, and special-purpose drives). Comparisons are made with previous years or drives. There is also a breakdown by use in the case of special-purpose gifts. An expectancy report showing how much can be expected from various sources according to prespecified probabilities assigned by the development office is periodically produced.

One of the great difficulties encountered in studying the financial problems and programs of higher education is the lack of comparable data. This difficulty is rooted partly in the variety of definitions of such "simple" terms as *student* or *faculty*. However, the same problem is often encountered within a single institution. The development of an automated accounting system rests not only upon a careful definition of the procedures to be followed to achieve specific results, but also upon common definitions of terms.

Among the questions which it should be possible to answer in any good financial system are:

What is the cost of instruction per student?

How does it vary by department?

What is our indirect cost rate and what does it include?

What does it cost to add a faculty member to the staff?

What is the cost to the library of accessing a book?

What would be the net effect on income if we raised tuition?

One comment on the problem of developing financial systems is germane: although each institution may (with some justification) regard its problems as unique, some of the elements of generally useful programs may be found in a great many institutions with similar equipment and procedures. It may not be necessary to design every computer program for such applications as payroll and accounts receivable as if the problem had never been encountered before. Those administrators who are in the process of developing financial systems may find considerable help in the publications and meetings of the College and University Machine Records Conference. Among all the possible administrative applications of computers, financial accounting is perhaps most easily adaptable for use by other institutions.[1]

In considering whether or how to establish a more effective financial processing and information system, the following comments are suggestive as well as typical of the need to be met:

A college is more like a business than most administrators are willing to admit —partly because they overstress the differences, but also because they don't know what business administration is really like.

We need *more* information than a business. We must be more reactive because of the animate nature of our products and materials. The analysis of day-to-day events is much more important. How can you improve the quality

[1] For a fuller discussion, see the chapter on automated data processing in the forthcoming revision of *College and University Business Administration* to be published by the American Council on Education.

of the product? The goals are undefined. Control and decision-making in academic administration are almost always ad hoc.

Administrators just aren't using enough of the sophisticated techniques of management. There is very little use on campus of faculty with mathematical, management science, or business administration knowledge. They could really help improve college administration procedures. Instead they are busy doing off-campus consulting. There is nowhere near the level of sophistication in using computers in the administration that there is in the academic ranks.

Every day we are asked to produce more and more information. Much of the demand comes from within, as we try to expand and to improve our own planning and operations. But state and federal agencies keep demanding new kinds of data. Professional groups and associations conduct surveys and want data. We're not equipped to furnish the information. For example, we don't have a complete file anywhere on our teaching and research equipment or on space utilization. Even when the information exists, usually in a file or combination of files, retrieval is time consuming and sometimes impossible. For our own sake, we ought to have data available on demand.

We simply have to use computers in administration. We want more up-to-date information and projections. Then, too, the job gets bigger and more complex, while our space, time, and personnel are severly limited.

Size is not the only criterion. Some of our best ideas come from small colleges. Their limited budget and limited sized equipment force them to be inventive.

One university is so squeezed for funds and so worried about its chances of survival that its trustees are borrowing private capital to speed up the development of an automated system of financial management. It is hoped that sufficient economies will result to repay the debt. Unfortunately there has been little useful research to justify the cost of data processing and computer systems solely on the grounds of possible savings. One of the difficulties, in addition to the short history of experience, is the fundamental incomparability of manual and automated methods. As one vice-president for finance said:

I'll be happy if we can hold our costs to what they are now. Manual accounting costs tend to go up with increased volume, but a computer can continue to handle more data without a proportionate increase in costs. I don't expect to be able to let any of our staff go, but I think we can hold the line against hiring.

Though there is little evidence to support the view that a mechanized system costs any less than a manual one which produces the same results, there is certainly widespread enthusiam about the improvement in the quality of the system when computers are introduced. The real dollar value of a more effective system is found in such by-products as improved planning, better support for budget requests, more effective controls, better use of scarce resources, and the release of some of the time of professional administrators from clerical drudgeries in favor of thinking, evaluating, and planning programs.

PROGRAM MANAGEMENT

Systems for handling student and staff records and for financial accounting and business management do not exhaust all of the administrative potentials of the computer. Many programs of concern to the administrator cut across the categorical boundaries of basic data systems or do not fit into neat cubbyholes. Instructional resource centers, for example, may have their own special needs, such as the scheduling of closed-circuit television, the distribution of audio-visual equipment and materials, the operation of language laboratories, and the preparation, scoring, and reporting of homemade tests and examinations. In some large institutions with extension divisions, automated methods of scheduling the distribution of sound motion pictures have been developed. Automatic inventory and scheduling of instructional resources facilitates access and use as well as optimum and convenient distribution, evaluation of effectiveness, ordering of materials and equipment, and planning for new services.

Many *libraries* have begun to make use of automated processes for ordering, acquisition, cataloging, and distribution. Even smaller libraries, using simple EAM (electromechanical accounting machine) systems, have found it more convenient to use machine-aided charge-out systems. The coordination of the special resources of multiple libraries on large campuses, or between members of statewide or affiliated systems, can be aided by computer systems. Much experimentation and research is still required to assess the feasibility of automated document search and retrieval, but the transactional systems of book ordering and cataloging, periodical control, and charge-out are clearly within the state-of-the-art of current data processing. Mechanized circulation records, projections of space requirements, improved recovery of fines and charges for loss—all are cited as advantages of automation in the library.

It has often been observed that librarians are among the last to become interested in automation. If this conservatism is indeed widespread, it may be understandable. Most libraries are short of funds and staff, many librarians were trained in an earlier day, and the task of conversion to automated procedures is in fact so overwhelming as to seem insoluble. Librarians hesitate to divert precious funds from books to machines and system development. The question of whether or not to automate, and to what extent, may be unavoidable, however, in view of the rapid growth of libraries and increased demands for their use. So few libraries have experimented with automation that it is difficult to generalize. It may be some time before it is safe to assert positively that libraries *must* automate if they are to survive the information explosion. But certainly the administrator should encourage those librarians who show an interest in pioneering in the field, even to the extent of such elementary applications as charge-out and circulation procedures.

Many *laboratories* in the usual instructional and research programs of the institution and those established for special outside research, sometimes at separate locations, need computers. The management of laboratories, observatories, nuclear reactors, agricultural experiment stations, or botanical gardens often involves information processing problems. Accounts and contracts may be separately managed, and sometimes the staff of the laboratory is not part of the general personnel system; cost accounting for laboratories may be especially tricky because of government auditing requirements. Planning the construction and operation of special facilities can also benefit from computer assistance. The scientific computer center may itself be considered a laboratory. In some institutions the operating system used by the computer contains an accounting system which automatically keeps track of the contract or project to which computer processing is to be billed. It is certainly anachronistic to find a manual bookkeeping system being used to keep track of the accounts of a computer center.

Keeping track of the administration of *university presses*, circulation figures for serial publications, mailing lists, billing, shipping can be assisted by an automated system, whether separate for the publications unit or as part of the general administrative system. (Some colleges treat extensive publication services and programs as affiliated institutions.) Research has been devoted to the development of automatic typesetting equipment, operated by a computer, and it seems very likely that these technological advances will affect the university or college press of the future.

In larger institutions *land and property management* may be a major enterprise. Some require the operation of full-time real estate and land management offices. The development of industrial park programs, in which the university leases land to selected commercial and industrial groups, may involve use of an extended data base, both for development and current operations. For example, one state university derives a substantial portion of its income from rentals on select property located in a nearby metropolitan center. The efficiency with which such enterprises produce revenue may be affected by the efficiency of data management for administrative purposes.

The *health services programs* of many institutions involve extensive records of patients, clinical services, and staff. The current management of such services is often a major enterprise. In addition, an automated data system provides valuable information for research, student personnel services, and planning for future needs and services.

In short, it seems difficult to imagine a program management problem for which the computer or an automated information system is not relevant. Even in a museum the cataloging of collections of manuscripts, art and artifacts, or specimens may involve extensive data management problems, not only for administrative purposes, but for improvements in cataloging, accessions, and the organization of a retrieval system for research and display.

COMPUTERS AND DECISION-MAKING

In what major ways does the computer system assist the administrator in making decisions regarding current and future operations? In a well-integrated system which includes data from most areas of concern to the president, the automated system has the following obvious advantages:

It can supply *live data*, with minimum reaction time between questions and answers and with increased assurance that the data reflect very recent if not current status.

It can (and should) reduce the volume of information through exception reporting—by reflecting only matters that need attention, by clear graphical displays or projections, and by sophisticated treatment which reduces multivariate data to univariate form whenever possible.

It provides for trial runs and simulation of decisions by automatic projections of the probable effects of present trends and experimental studies of the effects of policies prior to commitment.

It demands explicit declaration of policies, principles, and criteria for the design of the program—a demand which is sometimes as helpful as the system which follows from it.

It permits delegation of automatable rule-following controls. (If a rule can be explained and written out, a computer can follow it.)

It helps lower-echelon administrators take corrective actions as needed, without explicit intervention or constant surveillance at higher levels.

It provides hard facts to negotiate disputes and clarify the effects of alternative actions.

It is extremely important for the administrator to understand this proposition: *The computer never makes decisions. It carries them out.* The *decisions* are made when the system is designed—decisions to gather specified kinds of data from particular sources, to examine alternatives and take appropriate actions, to compare current status against criteria, and to create danger signals when things go wrong. It seems very unlikely that all decisions can ever be effected by computers, and hence the administrator is not likely to be displaced.

So many decisions require subjective evaluations, difficult to pre-
specify, or require dealing with the unexpected or fortuitous. Furthermore, at least within the present state-of-the-art, the administrator is
most critically important in borderline or mixed cases. For example,
the admissions officer can receive much help from a computer program designed to reduce data about an applicant to manageable
form. The applicant whose high school record, test scores, and other
data all suggest outstanding potential (or the complete reverse) provides no problem compared to that of the applicant with a miserable
high school record, outstandingly high College Board scores, glowing
letters of praise from the counselor, and a record of juvenile delin-
quency. The admissions officer will have to look the candidate in the
eye, evaluate the record by methods even he cannot explain, and
come to his own, partly subjective, decision.

Decision-Delegation

The role (and limitations) of the automated system can perhaps
best be illustrated by the kind of ad hoc automated system almost
any administrator sets up to deal with daily problems. The following
set of instructions by an administrator to his secretary is analogous
to a program for a computer:

Miss Jones, I'll be in Chicago all day tomorrow at the Palmer House. If Professor A calls and says his contract went through, I want to know, but if it

didn't I don't want to hear his excuses till I get back. If Professor B calls, ask him whether he decided to hire Candidate X. If he did, send the man a telegram—the usual one—from me; if he didn't, send him the usual letter. If you try to reach me at the Palmer House and they say I'm not there, you have my brother's home phone, try me there, but only if the Chairman of the Board calls. If the architect calls and says the bid was under $100,000, tell him to go ahead; otherwise, tell him I'll call him when I get back. If anybody else but my wife or the governor calls, take the message. If Dean C gets back from Europe tomorrow, have him chair the weekly meeting in my absence; otherwise, cancel the meeting.

All of the actions taken by Miss Jones in following the rules set forth in this typical case represent decisions made by the president. Cancelling the meeting (or not) does not depend on Miss Jones but only on the contingencies specified. Cases which are not amenable to the rules laid out are covered by such general rules as *"Take the message."*

The degree to which decisions can be defined for delegation to a computer, or to a lower echelon, is governed only by the degree to which the rules can be specified and the contingencies foreseen—and perhaps also by the quality of the data. Thus in telling the comptroller what he wants in exception reporting for budget control purposes (Miss Jones is here replaced, ultimately, by the system analyst who lays out the work for the computer programmer), the president could set forth his requirements as follows:

For this budget reporting system you're setting up, I want the following rules to apply:
1. Every Tuesday I want to know, by program and department, whether any current operating expense account has exceeded its budget by either 3 percent or $10,000—or has underrun by more than 5 percent or $20,000.
   a. The exceptions are the fertilizer study in the agriculture department, anything under the supervision of Professor D, or any work we're doing for the Atomic Energy Commission.
   b. Another exception would be any project under $150,000 in total budget for the year—or over $5 million in the case of underruns.
2. In each case, I want the overrun or underrun annualized as of the current date, and I want the report to show whom to call on what extension.
3. For any account, no matter what the size of the discrepancy, I want reports by May 1 on any monies which will revert to the state general fund if we don't spend them by the end of June.

In the foregoing, the president is not surrendering any of his prerogative as decision-maker. Instead, he is calling on the computer system for assistance in helping him devote his time to more difficult matters. He is explicit about the problems he wishes to deal with, and he may deal very subjectively, in the final analysis, with the situations to which the system alerts him. For example, he may call Professor D and find that the week's overrun is perfectly understandable—and hence give orders to revise the budget or provide additional assistance. He can revise his rules at will; for example, he could have added to his specifications more refined requirements to uncover trends:

Whether or not any budget underruns or overruns by these limits, I want to see a flag on anything which runs over or under for four consecutive weeks, no matter how small the percentage or amount.

The rules he establishes may apply to other personnel:

Every time there's an overrun of more than (some stated limit), I want the comptroller to run down the reasons and give me a report within 24 hours, with suggestions for action and supporting reasons.

Management Reports

The nature of the reports demanded or used by an administrator is usually determined by his most recent experience. If he has received typed reports from manual inputs, he will expect similar ones from the computer. If he has received reports from a punched card EAM system, reports from a computerized system will be expected to be similar. The capacity to generate reports and studies which fully exploit the potentials of a well-designed computerized system, with integration across all relevant programs and departments, depends partly on the administrator's understanding of what it is possible to ask for and of the rules of the game—hence partly on the ability of the computer system technician to communicate to the administrator what these potentials are in understandable and stimulating form. It was not an uncommon experience during the study reported here to find at the end of a day of interviewing that the president or key members of his staff had no idea of the breadth and flexibility—or, conversely, of the limitations—of the data base available to help them in their work.

The administrator must beware of making *defensive* use of data. One university president reported that his staff claimed their personnel resources were not keeping up with rising enrollments. An objective study showed that the only thing developing faster than the size of the administrative staff, relative to enrollment, was the national cost of living—and that there were many inequities and discrepancies among departments and branches. This study led to a reorganization —and it also muffled the malcontents. But it did not in itself answer the questions of whether growth had long been overdue, or whether needs differed justifiably, or whether future needs were being considered. The computerized system should not be used only to still the squeaking wheels.

At one institution, part of a statewide system, better data on class sizes and teaching loads led to the improvement of faculty salaries, though this college received the same funds for salaries as did other members of the system. In four years, this college rose from eighteenth among eighteen to fourth among twenty in its salary ranking, with an attendant reduction in average teaching load from 15 hours to 12 hours a week.

The benefits of computer-assisted decision-making are not limited to actual savings or internal improvements. Complaints about efficiency and economy may be legitimate, but we may sympathize with the public position of many administrators in dealing with those critics who do not understand their problems. As Francis E. Rourke and Glenn E. Brooks have pointed out:

One administrative vice-president remarked about the preparation of the university budget, "We simply use the displays that give us the best image." In this case, the image of quantitative rationality discharged the university's obligations to the state without reducing the scope of faculty control over academic policy. In such a crossfire between the demands of the academic community and pressures from the state, scientific management serves not so much to manage the university as to manage the impression that outsiders have about the university.[2]

The last comment may sound cynical, but any president who has struggled with external control agencies who do not see all his problems (or even want to) would be happy to have any assistance, even the legendary mendacity of statisticians, to obtain respite for real solutions to internal difficulties. Rourke and Brooks add that the "university has moved into a day in which, in order to obtain adequate financial support, it must reveal details about its operations that its president himself may not have known years ago."

[2] "The 'Managerial Revolution' in Higher Education," *Administrative Science Quarterly*, September 1964, p. 181.

The president who is not in command of the resources of the information system, or who does not know what a good system should be able to give him, is not in a commanding position to support his intuition by facts, much less to keep his fingers on the pulse of the institution beyond the level of fortuitous observation. What he observes is often determined by pressures of the day. He needs to know that beyond the opening and closing doors of his reception room lies a system which is quietly and effectively taking care of the daily grind while at the same time accumulating the life-blood of the decision process—facts which are current, dependable, comprehensible, accessible, and bound to come to his attention when he needs them, whether or not he knows he does.

On-going Planning

It cannot be too strongly emphasized that the use of an automated data base for projective and predictive studies, using a model of the institution based on studies of past experience plus inputs from faculty, administration, and students in the context of the supporting environment, should be an integral part of the information system and not something merely tacked on as a one-time institutional research project. The administrative staff should be able, as often as necessary, to answer such questions as:

Based on projections of enrollment, costs, facility utilization, and so on, what must we plan to do to meet our needs over the next x years?

Given our best guesses as to the steps we must take to meet the needs and achieve the goals we have defined, what is the most probable effect of actions a, b, c, . . . n? Group these effects into three ranges—optimistic, most likely, pessimistic.

At one institution, the demand for a four-year plan generated a systemwide study involving faculty and all administrative departments. Each faction was asked to define its goals in terms of expansion or contraction, levels of quality, cost ranges, staffing and facility needs, and the like. In a supporting action, the administration gathered historical and environmental data and prepared a computerized model for each program phase. The results were then discussed in a "trialogue" among trustees, administrators, and faculty leaders to form the basis for decisions about policies and actions to effect them. They expressed the results of the study in terms of a series of ratios: student/faculty, student/administration, faculty/administration, cost/student, floor space/student, office space/faculty, endowment/student. Some of these ratios were descriptive; others defined goals for development campaigns, cost reduction programs, building designs, and land acquisition. As experience showed the effectiveness of developing such a vocabulary for problem-definition and the design of specific programs, the college decided not to limit this procedure to a one-time study but to repeat it periodically, correcting the model and redefining goals as experience showed whether or not the model adequately reflected the effects of the new program.

Such an interactive system, permitting continuous monitoring of the current program as well as ensuring that future needs are under continuous scrutiny, can be of inestimable value to the president and his staff. From time to time, it is possible to ask: How are we doing with respect to goal y? How far are we falling behind or exceeding our expectations? Should we change the goal to fit this year's experience, or devote more effort to achieving it? Have we done so well in this area that we can divert more time and energy to goal z? Do we need to adjust the probability estimates we attached to various portions of the model? Have the weights we attached to various considerations proved to be good estimates of their importance?

The number of factors to be considered in planning, setting tuition and wage levels, establishing optimum student-faculty ratios and class sizes, calculating the effect on per student income from fixed endowments in the face of rising enrollments, may lead to quite complex formulas, with many fixed and variable parameters. It may be difficult to visualize how they will interact even if they are written out. With the aid of computer-produced data including computer-plotted graphs, it may be possible to find optimum limits for enrollment or maximum payoffs for shifts in resource allocations. For example, such questions as the following (fairly simple) one may be expressed in terms of mathematical relations:

Assuming that income-producing endowment remains fixed, the endowment income per student must decline with rising enrollments. Assuming that the cost of instruction can be fixed at a point at which increased cost of faculty per n additional students can be recovered by the additional tuition revenue, at what enrollment level will the income per student from endowment fall below the total cost per student of the institution's operations?

Data do not always behave in a nice linear fashion—each increment of another student costing or returning the same amount. Overhead rates may decline or increase with varying size. Often the administrator wants to optimize several things at once—keep costs per student to a minimum, maximize the use of faculty time, serve a prescribed number of students in the community, reduce overhead. Even when good data are available for use in prediction, it is difficult to know how they will interact, when a particular projection will reach a bend point and begin to decline rather than increase. The use of such operations research techniques has yielded great savings in business, industry, and government.

Wherever planning must be done in the face of uncertainties and of many variables whose relationships cannot easily be expressed along a single dimension, the computer comes to the administrator's aid and tries to point up in bold relief the most foreseeable consequences of his apparent alternatives. The computer does not replace the administrator, nor does it rob him of his essential work of decision-making. On the contrary, it permits him to study, in terms he can comprehend, the effects of judgments made in domains whose complexities are beyond the power of the human mind to manage. The computer supplements but does not supplant the human processes involved in the subtle balancing of unfathomable uncertainty and incomplete information which characterizes the world of administration.

5

ACADEMIC SERVICES

ALTHOUGH THE COMPUTER is becoming an important tool of academic administration, its key role remains in serving the academic community. Four principal sources of motivation behind the growth of the computer in the educational program are commonly cited:

1. The growing demand for computer services in academic research in a growing number of disciplines;

2. The need in an increasing number of fields to use the computer as a professional tool after graduation;

3. The growing demand for computer scientists and technicians in all major occupational sectors; and

4. A concommitant growth in interest in research and development in the computer sciences and related disciplines.

Computer technology and the information sciences have begun to figure prominently in almost every major scientific, professional, and social enterprise. The significance of this fact must be grasped by those who seek to maintain a responsive relation between higher education and the environment which supports it and which it seeks to serve. It is no exaggeration to say that the computer has had a revolutionary effect on research in the areas where it is already widely used. It promises to affect profoundly both content and method in education. In becoming useful and even indispensable in so many different ways on the campus, computer technology is becoming one of the twentieth century's key educational inventions, one which may affect the whole academic community and its intellectual life.

The remainder of this chapter is devoted to a brief survey of the academic uses of computers, and particularly to four aspects of their use:

1. As a tool of *research*;
2. As a *subject* of research;

3. As a subject of *instruction;*
4. As a *tool* of instruction.

A TOOL OF RESEARCH

The earliest and still most frequent use of the computer is for the analysis of quantitative observations—statistical summaries, univariate and multivariate analyses, the numerical solution of sets of equations plotting of graphic data, and a host of methods of data analysis and reduction. The principal value of the computer in such applications is its ability to handle masses of data with great speed and precision and to perform laborious and iterative calculations which are tedious or impractical for manual processing even with the aid of desk calculators.

This simple ability of the computer to perform many calculations has extended the ability of the researcher enormously—one writer has compared its effect to that of the power tractor on farming. A college faculty member says that the availability of the computer has extended his working career from 30 to 300 years: in reducing the time spent on routine, it leaves him ten times the opportunity for the creative aspects of his research. However, the computer in research is not without its attendant dangers. Research at the frontier may mean delay in performing actual experiments. The development of programs for the analysis of experimental processes requires numerous man hours. Unfortunately, some scholars tend to let the computer process become an end in itself, do little else but program, and neglect the implementation of experimental results. For some the computer is a fascinating toy; it then becomes a trap. Once data are obtained *the researcher is not absolved of the responsibility of interpretation.* This the computer cannot do. Careful planning must precede and painstaking review must follow the use of information to ensure that it is directly related to research questions. Used with care, the computer can reduce data to manageable proportions; an overabundance of data may give the researcher mental indigestion and actually hamper his research.

In the hard sciences, heavy dependence upon numeric calculations has resulted in extensive use of computers. In high-energy physics and in engineering, the central role of the computer is well recognized. In other areas of study, the introduction of the computer has done more than simplify the chore of doing calculations. Because of what it makes possible, altogether new methods of approach are being introduced. In meteorology, for instance, mathematical methods of weather prediction require complex and detailed computations. Such applications tax even today's largest computers but may become commonplace as the capacity and speed of computers continue to increase. It has also proved efficient to connect computers directly to other tools of observation—or to the object of observation itself. Computers not only can observe phenomena in an atomic reactor but also can be used to control them.

In the life sciences, now only a little less mathematically oriented than physics and chemistry, the computer has not been used as soon nor as extensively, though such usage has increased rapidly for several reasons. The growing importance of such interdisciplinary fields as biochemistry and biophysics has impelled many biologists to use methods analogous to those of physics and chemistry. The increasing use of electronic devices for observation (in neurophysiology and brain research, for example) has created voluminous files of data which demand computer analysis. Additionally, with some intervening means of translating raw responses into digital form, neurologists, for example, may hook electrodes to nerve cells or the cerebral cortex, with responses going directly into the computer.

In biology, as in physics and chemistry, the computer is beginning to affect the kinds of research that are performed and the kinds of new questions that scientists may ask. The capability of the computer to analyze vast accumulations of data tirelessly and relatively cheaply makes it possible to investigate matters which have been heretofore too complex for simple analysis—in particular, research into events involving many long, frequent, or simultaneous observations.

This capability of computers (manipulating vast numbers of observations) has made the computer a welcome addition to the tools at the disposal of behavioral and social scientists. In the dependence of certain methods on sampling and statistical techniques, the computer has been a natural ally. A development of considerable importance in the social sciences (and elsewhere as well) has been the use of computer-based simulations. The technique of simulation is certainly not new. In engineering the use of models has been commonplace for many years—scale-model airplanes flown in wind tunnels are a familiar example. The computer makes possible different sorts of models, some of which do not physically resemble their real-world analogues, but in which significant aspects of the real world are represented mathematically. This technique has obvious applications in engineering (replacing, in some cases, the scale-model techniques), but the implications for the social sciences are only beginning to be realized. Computer models can be built of social systems, of any system indeed that can be described mathematically. An economic or political system, for example, can be simulated; using this tool, the economist or political scientist can ask hypothetical questions about the behavior of social systems under various conditions and influences.

Such recent developments as time-sharing make it possible to use simulation in a highly interactive context, one in which the participant in a dialogue with the computer obtains answers, estimates, projections, and the like almost immediately. The simultaneous use of several remote response terminals makes it possible for a group of men to interact with each other and with a shared computer in an environment designed by humans but generated, monitored, paced, and recorded by the computer. At this point in research, it has been observed, the simulated system becomes an instructional device (and we spill over into another subject of this chapter); however, the instructional and instructive use of research is nothing new.

In the humanities the use of computers has until now largely been peripheral, assisting the researcher in the manipulation of information ancillary to his research per se. The production of indices and concordances is the most frequent aspect of this work. In an area growing out of this manipulation of text (called stylistic analysis) the computer is used to compile figures characterizing style (sentence length or structure, use of imagery, caesura, and feminine ending in verse). Styles of different authors (or of known authors and questionable works) can then be compared. Another use has been made of computers by humanists: to simulate artistic creation. Beatnik poetry, abstract paintings, and music composed by computer appear occasionally in the news and seem like an innocent (but rather expensive) game. Their real value, however, is as simulations. In music, for instance, a scholar may feel he understands the rules of musical compositions and the place of choice or random processes. Building a computer program embodying this understanding, he can learn how complete and adequate his rules are through evaluation of the output. There are other reasons, of course, for the use of computers in such chores as production of music and poetry: to learn more about computers and what they are capable of; but this takes us into computers as the *subject* of research.

A SUBJECT OF RESEARCH

When one speaks of conducting research in computers and computing, one may mean anything or all things along a broad spectrum of studies, from the engineering design of computers and computer components to the mathematical and logical investigations of information theory and the theory of automata. The rapid development of the computer field in its short history has obviously been the result of considerable research in the design and production of computers as pieces of hardware. In the early days, computers were designed by engineers. At times the theory of computing barely kept ahead of the production engineers. As human beings were faced with problems of programming there was inevitably some feedback from users to producers, and the characteristics of machines were increasingly tailored to make it easier for humans to use them.

Computer programming in the earliest systems was seen as a craft with little attempt to consider it as more than a means to an end. In some large systems, however, it was discovered that programming soon made expensive and time-consuming demands on the system; some consideration had to be given to doing it faster and more cheaply. Gradually, new tools (languages for programming, aids for program testing, and so on) were developed; modifications were made to the computers themselves to make them easier to use. These developments eventually resulted in some interest in the theoretic aspects of computers and programming. There were attempts to understand and describe formally, in the language of mathematical logic, computers and computer languages.

Although some of this work is quite abstract, much of it has some practical use. Support for such research has come largely from agencies interested in accelerating the development of computer technology. For example, there is considerable research in formal descriptions of computer languages and in the general nature of compilers

—the programs that translate the language written by the user into the language of the computer. One of the goals of such research is the automatic construction of compilers (now one of the most complex types of programs written), so that one would have only to prepare a formal description of the two languages involved to produce a compiler. There are many other types of research in the area of software—natural language processing, data-file organization and sharing techniques, visual character recognition and analysis by computers, methods of translation and content analysis applied to linguistic data, simulation and gaming, the mathematical theory of algorithms, information abstracting, storage and retrieval, techniques of numerical analysis, and a growing variety of topics the names of which are themselves of relatively recent origin in some cases.

There is a growing body of research (and much more is needed) in the use of computers—in man-machine systems, the development of programming systems, interactive use of computers, theories of programming, higher-order languages, the use of networks of computers and commonly shared data banks, and the application of networks of computers to process control. Research into such problems as the simulation of thought process and human learning and the attempts to teach computers to profit by their own experience represent hybrid cases of computers used as both a subject and a tool of research. It has already been demonstrated that in a primitive sense computers can learn, can program themselves, and can design and produce other computers.

Then, too, there is the general field of research in the role of computers, and of robots and automata in general, in social, political, economic, and general systems. Those conducting such research may develop still more applications and needs for research.

These examples, by no means exhaustive, have dealt largely with the theory and practice of using computers. Large research efforts are also devoted to the construction of computer hardware. It is difficult in this research to distinguish closely between theory and practice; many university scientists would call the work development rather than research. Indeed, the largest research efforts in physics and engineering aspects of computing are performed by hardware manufacturers rather than at colleges and universities. The search for materials, fabrication methods, and system organizations that will make computers larger, faster, and cheaper has been one of the most phenomenally successful research efforts in modern technology.

A SUBJECT OF INSTRUCTION

As the computer rapidly becomes an integral part of American civilization, instruction programs, designed to accomplish three major objectives, are needed: (1) to train professionals to use the computer as an essential tool of their trade; (2) to train computer specialists to meet growing technological demands; and (3) to make computers familiar tools to *all* students living in an increasingly automation-oriented culture.

Training Professionals

For students in such majors as business, psychology, and science it is highly desirable that they learn the rudiments of computers and computer programming. The future will require such knowledge. Work on current studies and research can be greatly faciliated. In one small college many undergraduates must do thesis work involving the computer. As an example of the creative outcome of this curricular requirement, a mathematics and an English major jointly wrote a computer program that would produce poetry after the model of the French imagists. To those students who see direct application of computing to their academic major, computer science means more than merely identifying concepts or formulating algorithms. Growing skill in this field enables them to deal more successfully with the logical structuring of problems. In addition, they often have gained an added measure of respect for the careful synthesis and analysis required in problem-solving.

Some campuses do not offer formal courses but feel it is the responsibility of each individual department to train its own students. For instance, people in the chemistry department who know computing are considered best qualified to teach their colleagues and students about chemical data processing. Arguing for a separate department of computer science, with development of this area as an independent discipline, implies to some that such a group would be free to determine best approaches to all similar computational work on campus. Without such a synthesizing group, those faculty members with the interest and ability would be scattered about the campus with an attendant unevenness in computational standards and in some cases a real waste of scarce human resources.

Training Computer Specialists

The fact that over 80 percent of the world's computer systems are installed in the United States underscores a major responsibility of America's higher education institutions. Initially most computer science training courses were offered by the computer manufacturers as on-the-job training. Subsequently formal course sequences and majors in computer science have evolved within the university framework primarily in such departments as engineering, mathematics, or business management.

Many junior colleges and small four-year colleges find that training is the major justification for their acquisition of computers. The need for programmers, analysts, and computer operators in industry has placed pressure on these colleges to produce trained personnel to meet the demand. One junior college, without a computer of its own, is given free computer time by local industries anxious to have the college produce trained programmers they can hire.

Undergraduate programs today must give students a foundation for work in the computer sciences, enabling them: (1) to qualify for employment as programmers, analysts, as members of the service teams in large-scale computer operations; and (2) to develop competence for further study in fields in which the computer is needed. One large university is providing this professional training under the auspices of the Department of Electrical Engineering. Courses presently reach undergraduates by closed-circuit television, with nine full-time equivalent instructors involved in teaching. Hands-on experience is provided in the computer research center where a faculty member and a number of graduate assistants offer guidance.

A rapidly increasing number of institutions is establishing programs in computer science. One recent count indicated that doctorates were offered at fifteen institutions in the United States and master's degrees at more than thirty. Such programs are sometimes offered by departments of computer science; more often, they are interdisciplinary programs involving mathematics, electrical engineering, and other related disciplines. Perhaps because of its interdisciplinary nature—and certainly because it is very new and little understood—

there has been some doubt expressed whether there even is such a thing as computer science.

The *future* impact of computers upon science curricula is very dependent upon the nature of the development of computer science and whether or not it becomes a widely accepted discipline. The subject . . . is still in a formative stage, and . . . it will likely remain unclear for some time yet as to whether or not it will ever reach full maturation as an independent academic discipline. . . . Probably the only way in which the academically correct position for computer education can be determined is for a few bold and affluent institutions to go ahead with a computer science program and see what a few years' experience brings.[1]

Some institutions consider computer science as part of a broader area of research, calling it information science. Students in these schools would expect to study linguistics, social psychology, epistemology, and operations research, in addition to mathematics, engineering, and computer design and application per se. Such a program may appear as close to library science as it is to computer science. In this broader context, the following definition may be enlightening:

Computer science is concerned with *information* in much the same sense that physics is concerned with energy; it is devoted to the *representation, storage, manipulation* and *presentation* of information in an environment permitting automatic information systems. As physics uses energy transforming devices, computer science uses information transforming devices.[2]

General Education

Leaders in a growing number of colleges realize that perhaps all students should learn something about computers. These devices are coming to play such a large role in every citizen's life that it may be important that everyone understand at least the rudimentary theory and practice of computation. The intent of such a program is not to provide technical training in addition to (or in place of) a liberal arts education. It is rather to provide an education in response to two factors: (1) the majority of today's college graduates will sooner or later in their careers have something to do with computers, and (2) automation generally (and the computer in particular) is creating many new social problems which can only be solved

[1] Gordon R. Sherman in *Proceedings of the Ninth College and University Machine Records Conference 1964*, p. 61.

[2] "An Undergraduate Program in Computer Science—Preliminary Recommendations," *Communications of the ACM*, VIII, No. 8 (September 1965), 544.

by informed people. Understanding what automata are, and of what they are capable, is a crucial part of this information.

Many institutions are seriously considering making a programming course compulsory for all students; a few have done so. The lack of qualified instructors and the pressures of competing curricular requirements make such a move difficult for any college. Yet many feel such courses offer the only acceptable introduction to the world of computers. J. C. R. Licklider remarks: "I think the first apes . . . decided that learning language was a deadly bore. They hoped that a few apes would work the thing out so the rest could avoid the bother." [3] He then goes on to say something which expresses the feeling of many academicians interviewed in this study:

Although the first immediate concern of the university may properly be with the education of students, the education of students may not be the best focus within which initially to examine the computer's role. It may be better to consider first the whole domain of creative intellectual processes (which is, I think, the proper domain of the university) and to ask what role the computer may play in that process. [4]

A TOOL OF INSTRUCTION

Scientists and scholars who find the computer valuable in their research will want their students to use it. They will present problems of a complexity that makes hand calculation impossible. Many instructors feel that this has had a vastly liberating effect on teaching; instead of trivial and contrived problems with many simplifying assumptions, real-life problems can be presented to the student. In engineering, the availability of computers is modifying the curriculum significantly at many institutions; in one case, an engineering professor now gives freshmen exercises which were given as senior projects a few years ago.

The availability of the computer has decreased the tedious pencil-pushing demands of mathematics and has allowed (or forced) students to look beyond the mere manipulation of symbols to mathematics as a tool of thought. Paradoxically, the computer is often thought of as a tool of mathematics, but it is rarely used by mathematicians. The processes of applied mathematics are so readily per-

[3] In Martin Greenberger, ed., *Computers and the World of the Future* (Cambridge: The M.I.T. Press, 1962), pp. 203-4.

[4] *Op. Cit.*, pp. 205-6.

formed by the computer that the mathematician has often turned to more theoretic pursuits.

The use of computer-based simulations has also proved to be a powerful teaching tool. A system which the students are to study is simulated. The students then explore this simulated system, testing it under varying conditions as they never could the real system. Perhaps the most widely known example is "management games" (simulations of business organizations). The students "manage" the organization and see the effect of alternative policies on production, sales, profit, etc.

An Environment for Learning

In a very special sense, a computer provides an environment for learning. It also can be used to control associated environments. *The computer can, with proper programming, teach its users to use it.* In modern programming systems, the computer provides either gratuitous or requested comments, explanations, and error flags. Many people who learn programming and who use computers for the first time find the experience almost esthetically satisfying, sometimes to their great surprise. On many campuses one can hear stories about students who become computer addicts, so interested in computing that they suffer seriously in their other course work.

It is important to understand some elements of this phenomenon in order to see some of the reasons why, to many people, the computer seems to have such a powerfully potential value as an aid to instruction. The following is a fairly typical explanation offered by an instructor interested in the reasons for the fascination of the computer to some users:

First, there's the attraction to bright students in problem-solving. Unlike most instructors, the computer responds *right now*. If you leave out a left parenthesis in an expression, the computer lets you know at once. If you fail to define something that has to be defined, the computer notices it with unerring speed. The whole process is highly responsive, and the rewards for correct work are immediate, as in programmed instruction. If you get a process to run 10 percent faster, you almost feel it's like beating the slot machine—and you may save money. (One student compared it to writing music.) You set up a series of events, connected in a logical way, push the GO button, stand back, and then it all rolls along in beautiful order. You've put something together after a lot of thought and effort, and it works! If it doesn't, you get an objective and temperate reaction, including useful criticism. You get positive, clear responses (something you don't always get from humans), and while you're using the computer you have its undivided attention. You can exert your own will on it, and it does just what you tell it, with endless patience; if you tell it to do something incorrect, it does that, and then you have nobody but yourself to blame.

Computer-Aided Learning

Within the past decade, computers have begun to be used to teach many subjects other than their own use. For either linear or branched programmed instruction, the computer can recognize correct responses, branch from one part of a lesson to another according to student responses, prod the student (by ringing a bell or blinking a light) if he dawdles, signal the instructor if the student is having unusual difficulty, keep track of individual and group performance. The computer can also provide computational services—become an imitation desk calculator but with vastly increased power. In a course in statistics for example, the computer can generate data with prescribed frequency distributions and then permit the student to sample from these and estimate parameters. Early experiments revealed that it was possible to use the computer as an overgrown teaching machine; using time-shared remote terminals, several students can use the same program at once. Experiments have been tried successfully as far down as the primary grades, in which the same "slot machine" fascination seems to be exerted on many users. Visitors to experimental laboratories sometimes have to be dragged away from the machines on which they are trying demonstration materials.

Since computers can be designed to control a variety of devices, they can be used to turn audio-visual equipment on and off, advance a new frame in a slide projector, generate visual displays, check against elapsed time, and activate signalling devices. The present and projected uses of computer-assisted instruction and learning are being explored on an increasing number of campuses. The problems impeding further progress are expense of equipment, expense of developing software and course materials, noise of some types of equipment, and needs for better understanding of principles and methods. A further discussion of future potentials in this field is presented in Chapter 11.

6

GETTING STARTED

COMPUTERS ARE in many ways different from other kinds of equipment that colleges buy, rent, or use. There is perhaps no better way to examine the special role of the computer on campus than to look at the college which is in the process of acquiring a computer for the first time; many of the problems of choice that arise initially are indicative of the kinds of decisions that will have to be made all along the road.

During our study more than fifty representative colleges and universities were visited. No single model of wisdom was encountered. There are as many patterns of development as there are colleges; the technician working effectively in one environment might not be successful in another. The size, wealth, growth rate, and experience of the institution all have a bearing, as does the relative importance of teaching and research. Honestly told, the history of most first encounters with computers shows examples of errors in judgment, misunderstandings, and plans which could not be implemented.

The successful, valuable, and well-supported college computer center does not appear overnight. It results from careful planning, gradual development, and replanning. It may even be necessary to make mistakes; in some cases, there is no faster way to achieve insight. It requires a careful tailoring of the costs and capabilities of the computer center to the present and changing needs and resources of the college. And perhaps most important, it is the result of missionary work on the part of the first man on campus who sees the need for and the potential of the computer. It is often the result of considerable daring on the part of the man who first said, "Okay, let's do it."

PATTERNS OF DEVELOPMENT

Perhaps the most frequent pattern is for interest in computers to emerge from a definite circle of academic need. A few members of the faculty would like to use computers to support their research. In order to acquire the capabilities they need, they must stimulate a demand on the part of other faculty and administrators. They do this by teaching their colleagues what computers are and what they can do for them. A classic case reads somewhat as follows: An individual professor (examples include physicists, psychologists, chemists, sociologists, economists, geologists) uses the computer services offered the college by a neighboring university. Eventually, he finds this inconvenient and wants his own computer for research and instruction. He begins to persuade his colleagues that they could use the computer in their work, and eventually he educates a larger group of decision-leaders in the basics of computer technology. Finally, they present their requirements and recommendations to the administration.

One junior college was given an antiquated and unmarketable computer by a local industrial firm as a tax write-off. An instructor in electronics thought it would be interesting to get the machine running so that his students could see what a computer looked like. Once it was running he tried to find work for it. He managed to convince some of the other faculty and some administrators to do some of their statistical processing on the machine. Before long it was so overloaded that the college was forced to acquire a new and bigger machine.

Other pressures can lead the college into acquiring data processing equipment. The demand for computer training in the community may lead the college to offer courses in data processing. The continuous increase in paperwork may force administrators to consider data processing for economic reasons—or simply because there are not enough clerks available to keep all the ledgers and transcribe all the required reports. One administration which thought computers were very remote suffered a rude awakening when it was found that senior scientists and scholars were refusing the college's recruitment offers because of inadequate computing capability on the campus to support their research.

STARTING TOO BIG

The awakened administration must beware of starting too big. A large, shiny, and powerful machine may appear impressive, but an unused white elephant is hard to hide. It is a considerable embarrassment to let a machine whose price is measured in dollars per minute sit idle. It is safer to start small and plan to grow, even if it appears time and energy, and perhaps money too, are wasted by doing things twice. Such time and energy are invested in experience for which there is no substitute.

One state-supported four-year college felt it needed a computer to uphold its prestige. The legislature bought a computer, but no one planned the second step. Now, two years later, the machine is used only a few hours a day. Administrative systems use different machines; no money was in the budget for teaching students to use it; there was no plan to use computers for faculty research.

One cautious junior college began to use the data processing facilities of a nearby industrial firm. This allowed them to get acquainted with the problems, experiment and make mistakes, and acquire their own machine only when they knew what they wanted and needed and when enthusiasm had spread around until there was a wide enough circle of users to support a computer.

The wise administration profits by the mistakes of the computer pioneers; no college administrator today needs to look far in order to learn from the experiences of his peers. If the college administration wishes to take a quantum jump in the early stages, they may find it useful (and in the long run economical) to consider hiring experienced personnel at an early date or to use consultants for a short time. This serves to prevent costly mistakes and to educate the faculty community to face its responsibilities for leadership in the integration of computer facilities in the educational program. Some computer manufacturers provide excellent courses which make a fine introduction to data processing. Some manufacturers promise any amount of free help in analyzing the college's problems and requirements. This can be valuable, if it is remembered that the advice of someone with something to sell will not always be unbiased. One who feels the need for analysis and advice concerning his transportation problems would be wise to listen cautiously (if at all) to an automobile salesman.

ECONOMIC CONSIDERATIONS

With regard to computers and economics there are two kinds of college presidents: those who are afraid they are spending too much and those who are afraid they may not be spending enough. Both ask the same question: How much *should* we be spending on computers? There is only one sensible answer, but it is not very helpful —as little as possible.

The question of how much *should* be spent is not immediately answerable. To ask it too early is to indicate that the basic problems have not been well formulated. When the college first begins using computers, the amount that should be spent is of course very little, since there will be few users. As the number of users increases and the demands of some individual users increase, the amount will rise very quickly. In the long run, one may hope that computer costs will be analogous to those of a library. The college should not be extravagant but should spend enough to satisfy the faculty and students and maintain appropriate standing if not prestige. A small college requiring the image of high scientific competence may need to spend a great deal on computers. Larger schools may have other objectives and (unless also very scientifically oriented) may defer spending very much on computers at all. The amount of research—particularly funded research—will affect costs and expenditures. Some colleges will have extensive programs in computer science education; many will have none, at least for the next few years.

One thing must be made clear however: *the cost of the computer hardware is by no means the total cost.* Computer personnel will probably cost as much again. Although estimates vary widely, the generally accepted average is that equipment accounts for only about one-third to one-half of the cost of operation of a computer center. Other rules-of-thumb are cited frequently but tend to be unhelpful or unreliable unless carefully qualified. One is that a college should spend (say) one dollar per student per month on computing. In a brief test of this theory, it was found that colleges could be found who spent less than five cents and others which spent more than ten dollars. Another rule is that three (or one or two) percent of the college's operating budget should be devoted to computing. This guideline is also empirical: it is within the range one can establish by computing such a percentage at several colleges selected at random.

A bewildering diversity of budgeting practices can be seen which compounds the natural confusion in degrees of interest. Many colleges hide the extent of their data processing operation by supporting it from many different cost centers: the center itself has only a modest budget, because staff salaries are paid out of various department budgets. One large state university with a bewildering array of large, powerful, and expensive machines has an incredibly meager budget for computers. Since most of them are paid for out of research grants and contracts, they are not included in the budget published for the legislature.

If the college is interested in becoming involved in computing and is uncertain about economic feasibility, it might study the costs of using a computer at some other college or at a local industry at first. This is bound to be only a stopgap measure, however, until faculty and staff better appreciate what the computer is worth. Just as the college would not routinely send the faculty to the town's public library for books, it should not long expect the faculty to go off campus for vital computing services.

Representative Costs

The most recent issue of a widely used guide to current computers[1] lists machines qualifying as computers with monthly rentals from $500 to more than $250,000. Neither of these extremes will interest the average college. On the following pages are some examples of what colleges are now spending for computers. It should be noted that, in some cases, the figures presented here differ considerably from those to be found in the college budget. Salaries of personnel managing the computer center are frequently hidden in departmental budgets; amortization of purchased equipment is frequently ignored; the value of space used is almost never considered. The figures shown here are realistic estimates of real costs to the college. The amortization figures used are common in the computing industry—20 percent per year for computers and 15 percent for EAM. The percentage figure following each total is the approximate percentage of the total annual budget spent on computing.

College A is a small four-year college with an annual budget of approximately $2,000,000. Its curriculum is science-oriented; it has

[1] *Computer Characteristics Quarterly,* published by Adams Associates, Cambridge, Mass.

less than 500 students. The computer is used about 120 hours per month. Of this, administrative uses account for five hours, faculty research accounts for perhaps ten. The remainder of the time is used by the students. All students are taught programming; they are then encouraged to use the machine for their homework and independent study. The machine is small and relatively slow; faculty users frequently make use of larger industrial computers and those at other colleges. The annual budget for College A's computer includes:

Amortization of capital equipment	$10,000
Maintenance	3,400
Supplies	750
Personnel (student assistants)	2,000
Personnel (faculty time, estimated)	5,000
Total	$21,150 (1+%)

The center occupies the space of two average classrooms. An estimate of computer time used by faculty off campus is $5,000 per year.

College B is a public two-year college with 7,000 students. Its annual budget is approximately $21,000,000. The center contains a small computer—in fact the same model as College A. The center is operated approximately eight hours per day. Fifty to 60 percent of the time is used by students. Courses are taught in programming, operations, etc. The remainder of the time is used for administration, almost exclusively student and faculty record-keeping. Test scoring, analysis, grade reporting, and scheduling account for the bulk of the time. In addition to this center, the college uses more than 150 hours of computer time donated by local industry for instruction on a somewhat larger machine. College B's annual budget for its computer is:

Amortization of capital equipment	$ 6,000
Maintenance	1,200
Leased equipment	26,000
Supplies	3,000
Personnel (director, 2 clerks, student assistants)	20,000
Total	$56,200 (¼ of 1%)

The center occupies about 2,000 square feet. The value of the time donated by local industry is about $7,000 per year.

College C is a private university with 8,000 students and an annual budget of approximately $28,000,000. In addition to the medium-sized computer center described below, the university has a small center for administrative services and another for the medical school, which is isolated from the university. The major university computing center operates on two shifts, processing some two to three hundred jobs per day, serving approximately 500 students in the course of a year. Some fifty to one hundred faculty use the center for their research. Students use 40 percent of the time. The annual budget for College C is:

Amortization of capital equipment	$144,000
Maintenance of owned equipment	15,000
Leased equipment and supplies	100,000
Miscellaneous expenses	7,000
Salaries and wages (director, research scientist, system analyst, programmer, operations manager, computer operator, administrative assistant, clerk, part-time student assistants)	80,000
Total	$346,000 (1¼%)

College D is a state university with 25,000 students and an annual budget of approximately $90,000,000. The university computing center currently has four computers; of these, one is being phased in as another is being phased out. The center normally runs 2,000 to 3,000 jobs a day—although this can run as high as 5,000. At any one time about 4,000 job codes may be active. (A job code is the charging number for one program or set of related programs. One person may have more than one job code, and a job code may represent the work of more than one person.) About 32 percent of the available time is used by students; the remainder is used for research, except for a small amount of off-campus use. College D acquired its first computer ten years before this budget was written.

Amortization of capital equipment	$ 65,000
Rental of equipment	924,000
Supplies and materials	106,000
Personnel (15 professional, 19 clerical, 20 part time)	576,000
Miscellaneous (includes some remodeling of facilities)	100,000
Total	$1,771,000 (nearly 2%)

In addition, approximately $750,000 is budgeted for administrative data processing, bringing the total to almost 3 percent of the annual budget. This activity employs forty people and uses some leased equipment ($120,000) and the facilities of the computing center. The computing center occupies 12,000 square feet.

The smallest center described above, at College A, spends nearly $2,000 a month on computing. This is a small center; the computer is about as small as possible if it is to serve the students, faculty, and administrative staff in a generally useful way. Some colleges are considering a technique which will cut this figure in half. Access to commercial time-sharing systems is becoming increasingly available, particularly near larger cities. A college interested in obtaining limited amounts of computing power on a large and sophisticated system can obtain a terminal (consisting of a typewriter-like input/output device) linking it to one of these systems by telephone. The charge for such service may vary considerably, but the college can expect to pay less than $10,000 a year to receive such service, providing more computing power than is available to College A and infinitely more sophisticated software (particularly higher-order languages) to assist the users. The space requirements are obviously minimal, as are facility preparation costs. Unfortunately, the sheer volume of input and output involved in administrative data processing makes simple remote terminals less satisfactory for such use than for student instruction.

Sources of Funds

The private college first considers the possibility of finding a donor who will provide a computer as a partial or total gift. This is sometimes difficult to arrange. Computers are expensive and in some senses also somewhat impermanent. A donor is liable to have misgivings about a sizable gift which may be discarded as obsolete in a few years. However, if the college can present a convincing case for its need, it may be possible to attract funds for this purpose. In addition, even many obsolescent computers have some resale value, especially on the international market.

Funded research activities which will use the computer can be expected to pay for some part of the cost of operating the machine, but no more than a fair share. In the case of federal contracts, this share is very precisely determined. If the college can relate the acquisition of the computer to some essential and relevant need of the college, it may be possible to get a grant from a foundation or federal agency.

It has been suggested that the smaller college must justify the acquisition of computing equipment on the basis of instructional values. The local business community needs people trained in computer use, and if the college can help meet this need it may actively support efforts to acquire equipment to train personnel.

Total dependence on external funding, however, may reveal a failure to understand the role of the computer in the college. If the computer is recognized as an integral part of the educational program of the college, it is clear that it must be supported as is any other regular operating expense of the college. Alternative methods of budgeting such costs are discussed on pages 137-42.

Buy or Lease

Virtually all modern computers can be leased *or* purchased from the manufacturer. Many organizations have found purchase to be preferable, although it is an arrangement used less in colleges than in industry. In the literature of industrial management, there have been many discussions of the comparative advantages of leasing and purchase. In general, this indicates that the "crossover" is at about four years: that is, if an organization plans to keep a computer for more than four years, it is better to purchase; otherwise, one is better off to lease. In industry, of course, the problem is affected by tax and depreciation considerations, but a college faces different problems and must make its decisions on noncommercial criteria.

Many colleges have never considered leasing equipment of any kind and are opposed to the idea of leasing a computer. It seems preferable to view the computer as a single large item to be paid for at one time rather than as an expense continuing forever. This point of view, however, overlooks some important points. The computer is not a one-time expense. The cost of maintenance and personnel may equal the cost of the machine itself. The lifetime of a computer on the campus may be surprisingly short. As a rule, computers are superseded by better, faster, and more economical equipment in less than five years; also, in less than five years the computer may not be big enough, and a decision will have to be made to expand or replace it. It is worth noting that many large universities which have considerable experience with computers and who now use very large systems tend to lease rather than purchase equipment. A natural tendency seems to be to begin by purchasing, when the college is unsure of the role computing will play on campus, and then to lease when it is clear that computing has an important, continuing, and supportable future and/or when sponsored research agreements make it possible to recover a portion of leasing costs.

Each method of financing has its advantages and pitfalls. Some of the considerations which will affect the college's decision to lease or to purchase are:

1. *Source of funds.* The private college may find a donor who prefers to purchase a tangible object once and for all rather than to commit himself to long-term rental. The alternative is to try to educate the donor about the issues and persuade him to supply an endowment from which all or part of the rental can be paid. The problem of the publicly financed school is not essentially different. Legislative bodies frequently feel about the public's money much as the private donor feels about his own.

2. *Software investment.* Whether one buys or leases, the cost of replacement or expansion of capacity is not limited to hardware. As one president said, "The cost to users of the old computer, with their large investments in programming particular applications, is not only for reprogramming but for valuable time lost during a transition. These investments can run up to $100,000." One way around this is to bring in the new equipment and run it concurrently with the old system through the worst of the transition. The same president argued that the value of the old computer may be greater to the university than to a potential buyer because of its program library: "This dual life expectancy—the life over which the computer serves the university and the longer life over which it is almost necessary if essential research activity is not to be interrupted—lends a lot of weight to the argument for buying."

3. *Life expectancy.* If the college wishes to dispose of its purchased machine in a few years in order to replace it with a different one, it may find that it may be difficult to sell, even at a depreciated cost. An estimate should be made of the life expectancy of a computer and careful cost comparisons made of the different funding and amortization procedures.

4. *Replacement plans.* Another important consideration is the way in which the college's computer expansion requirements can be met. Most modern computers can be expanded by adding additional mem-

ory and peripheral units without replacing most of the original parts. Others—especially smaller ones—cannot be expanded and must be replaced in order to obtain a larger machine.[2]

5. *Mode of use.* If a computer is to be used primarily for a few projects which will continue indefinitely, the computer may be committed to those projects. When there is no longer enough spare time to satisfy other users, another computer (rather than a larger one) can be added to the center.

6. *Maintenance.* It is important to understand that a purchased machine involves a contract for maintenance services. This is often best provided by the manufacturer, whose personnel have the requisite training and access to parts, documents, and engineering facilities. It is seldom practical for any user, especially a small one, to maintain his own equipment.

Saving Money

Will the college reduce its administrative costs by using a computer? Probably not. A few comptrollers can point to actual minor savings, but in most cases this question is too complex to be answered either yes or no. Industrial organizations which have installed computers hoping that operating costs would go down have generally been disappointed—technically. As the administrator begins to learn what computers can do, he begins asking for things that were never done before because they were impossible. Hence cost comparisons are meaningless. If the college is content to have the computer do exactly what clerks now do and to see this go on unchanged and indefinitely, computers will probably save money in administration. But in the process of computerization, many antiquated procedures come to light and many new ways of doing things present themselves. Computerization almost always leads to modernization of procedures, redesign of methods, and an *increase* in the amount and kinds of work done. In the long run, especially in an expanding institution, overall savings will in all probability be provable. It is not uncommon to be told by a college official that its budget has doubled over a certain period of time while its (partially automated) administrative system cost has not increased anywhere near proportionately.

[2] See also the important comment about *"compatibility and flexibility"* on p. 94.

It is useful for the college president to speak of the *values* of a computerized system rather than of superficial *savings*. In such an argument the following points may be made:

With better information, he can plan more effectively and make better use of fixed resources.

With expanding enrollment and/or research programs, costs do not go up proportionally with volume.

Cost-of-living indices constantly force wages upward, while hardware costs remain relatively stable or go down.

If a machine does the work of n clerks, there is a reduction in such indirect costs as floor space, supervisory personnel, employee benefits, and training-retraining because of expansion and/or turnover.

It is difficult to place a precise dollar value on significantly improved quality of information, services, and planning.

Other Criteria

In establishing a computer center and the accessory systems to satisfy users' needs, the college must consider both hardware and software requirements and weigh the advantages and disadvantages of the systems available from several manufacturers. For example, if the software provided by the manufacturer is not adequate to the user's needs, he must create his own. Since the expert personnel needed to write compilers and executive programs are expensive, the cost of developing software must be added to the cost of the computer. Every piece of software which is provided by the manufacturer saves the user real (and sometimes much) money. Just as there are differences in quality among machines, there are differences in quality among software systems. For the FORTRAN language, for example, one manufacturer's compiler may assemble programs which run more efficiently (faster) than those of another, even on machines of comparable speed of operation.

It is important to emphasize at this point that the manufacturer should not be the sole source of information about the quality of his hardware and software. Whenever possible the opinions of those who have already used the machines and/or the software, preferably in comparable situations, should be solicited. The small cost of making comparative evaluations may be repaid many times over when the system is finally installed.

There are several crucial considerations which can be neglected only at great peril. A few of them are:

Reliability. Like most electronic gadgets, computers sometimes break down. Some have more of a reputation for this than others. The prospective buyer should be aware of these reputations; he should consult experienced users. There are measures of machine reliability in fairly common use: "mean time between errors" and "mean down-time" being two of the most meaningful (a machine is "up" when it is in use and working; it is "down" when it is out of service for repair or maintenance).

Maintenance. Closely related to reliability is hardware and software maintenance. How good will the engineers be who are going to keep the system going? Here again, the best source of information is another user. How far away will service personnel be? How long will it take them to get on the scene, once they are called?

Backup. Even the best of systems occasionally breaks down and requires hours of work to be repaired. It is in the nature of things that this happens only on the busiest days, when the payroll is due, on registration day, or when student use is heaviest. The college would do well to consider this situation before it arises. If the machine is to be used on such a tight schedule that a breakdown could cause a serious crisis, a comparable machine should be available somewhere nearby where programs can be run in an emergency.

Compatibility and flexibility. Because of the variations possible (adding more memory, different input or output devices, etc.) it is possible to increase or decrease the capabilities of the system considerably without replacing it. If the configuration proposed is as big as the central processor can possibly handle, there is no capability to expand. In such a case, if requirements increase, the entire system will have to be traded in on a larger one. The capability to move up (or down) in capacity and price may be very valuable, particularly when it is difficult to predict the rate of future growth.

A community of users. It may be important and valuable to share problems and programs with other institutions. The college may be able to take advantage of programs already written at another campus for admissions or fund accounting or budget projection. In the academic community, scientists and scholars frequently exchange programs; they will want to have the same machine that their colleagues have for just this reason. This is not simply prejudice (although this enters into it) but really a matter of convenience and economics. As the languages used in the administrative and academic communities become more available on more machines, this consideration becomes less crucial, but it is certainly worth consideration.

Programming assistance. The vendor will often offer to provide some "free" services to the new user. He will "lend the institution one or two programmers for a while" to help implement the first systems and to get things going. The college should be sure that it understands *exactly* what is being promised, how good the people will be, and *how long they will stay.* If the manufacturer is also willing to train personnel on the campus, this fact should also be spelled out. On the other hand, if these services are of no value to the college, this should be made clear to the vendor. *They are part of the price being asked.*

Competition. Computer manufacturing is a very competitive business, despite appearances to the contrary. The college should consider machines of several manufacturers and be quite frank with their representatives, letting them know that other manufacturers are on the scene. By comparing one potential system with another, the college representatives will get to know them all better, particularly their defects. Having several manufacturers' representatives to turn to, the college can be more assured of getting an unbiased picture of the situation and of the relative merits of the various proposals. Some colleges may play off one manufacturer against another in an attempt to get the best deal. It is worth the trouble to use the competition to get a full understanding of what is in fact being offered for the quoted price—particularly such extras as service or programming assistance. Even after the machine has been installed, both the college and the vendor should understand that the equipment can be replaced as better machines and services appear. Vendor services sometimes decline in quality if the vendor feels that he has a sure thing for an indefinite future.

7

A PLAN OF ACTION

THE COLLEGE PRESIDENT authorizing the acquisition of a new computer (particularly the first computer) is well advised to prepare a detailed plan of action. Five distinct tasks need to be considered. These are not successive steps to be performed one after the other. There will be some interaction among the tasks, and some overlap in time is inevitable. These tasks, done with warranted care and caution, take surprisingly long. The order in which the tasks are listed here may not be the order in which they will be done; it is the order in which it is easiest to describe them:

Estimate system requirements for a period of years.

Acquire and/or train personnel.

Select and install hardware.

Design an operating system and software.

Provide orientation for the user community.

THE STEP BEFORE THE FIRST

When sufficient interest exists on the campus to consider the acquisition of a computer, a computer committee (or task force) is usually organized to undertake or oversee the whole process. It is not unusual for such a committee to deliberate for a year or longer before recommending positive action on the part of the president. Unless the members of the task force have some prior experience, they will have to spend a considerable time in becoming educated about the issues, facts, and alternatives. To be really effective in their job, the committee members are as highly placed in the administrative hierarchy as possible, with a chairman reporting directly to the office of the president or vice-president. The latter himself charges them with their responsibilities and holds them accountable for their recommendations. The committee members represent those various faculty groups and administrative offices who are expected to be the major users of the computer. If there are technical specialists on the campus (often in an engineering school) who have some prior knowledge of or experience with computers, their help and advice should be sought. This principle seems obvious but is frequently violated. The committee is usually made up of members of the power structure whom the president trusts to provide the basis for his major decisions. Individuals with knowledge but no power are sometimes not only ignored but specifically excluded. It seems to be felt that people who know something about computers will be undesirably biased.

Getting Help

Many of these steps will be difficult for the college to undertake without help, especially if the committee members are experiencing their first exposure to computers. Consultants may seem an expensive luxury, but in the long run they usually prove to be less costly than the results of poorly conceived plans and premature or incorrect decisions. *A consultant should not be asked to make the decisions for the college or to do any of the tasks outlined here.* He supplies the needed technical information, explores the consequences of various alternatives with the decision-makers, and helps them to define and focus attention on important issues. Having outside support of this kind in no way diminishes the authority and responsibility of those designated to make recommendations and final decisions. A consultant serves as a technical resource to the persons responsible for making the decisions. He can spell out the alternatives, and the consequences, costs, and advantages of the alternatives, but he cannot interpret which one best suits future plans or suitable allocation of resources for the project. Colleges that have already developed successful computer facilities are often able to recommend experienced consultants, and the advice of these other institutions should be sought in locating them. Many institutions have found it wise to avoid the "free" consultants provided by computer manufacturers; even when it is a foregone conclusion that a certain vendor will be used, the cost of following his "free" advice may be excessive.

ESTIMATE REQUIREMENTS

The committee first considers what computer services the college can or should provide for students, faculty, and administration. Only then can they specify a computer facility adequate to those needs and translate the required capability into costs. It cannot be overstressed that a committee which begins by considering what the college thinks it can afford, or what specific pieces of hardware it would be desirable to have, is headed for trouble. Discussion must begin with a review of the specific requirements that are to be satisfied by the computer facility. This discussion should be reopened and reexamined throughout the study at regular intervals.

This committee faces a difficult assignment. Its job cannot be accomplished without deep involvement in many details which members will not be aware of or understand when they begin. In larger institutions, it may be necessary to charter a subcommittee of one or more people to work full time in estimating total computer system requirements. Whether the committee divides up the work among its members as a part-time enterprise or has one or two of its members work full time, answering questions like the following are characteristic of this phase and involve extensive interviewing and written communication:

What facilities are now used? By whom? How often? On what charge basis?

Which members of the faculty and administration have expressed interest in or need for computer services? What do they estimate to be their needs in terms of size and speed of the machine? Frequency and periodicity of use?

If there is a similar or comparable college within reach, what have they learned about demands for computer services? (It is undoubtedly worth the small cost to send a visiting team from the committee to spend a day or more at such institutions.)

Which members of the faculty and administration have *not* expressed any interest in computers who probably *will* once the center is in operation? (The basis for such assumptions may be logical or historical. The history of other institutions may be the best guide.)

What are our plans for expansion of student body, faculty, research facilities? What will be needed to support research work for which funds are now being solicited?

From common sense and from the observation of comparable

institutions, what can we estimate concerning the volume of computer work each year for the next five years?

Everything will not be converted to the computer overnight. In what sequence do we envision various applications (payroll, student records, scheduling) being added? What are the estimated volumes of work to be processed at what intervals?

How much time must be allowed for computer program checkout, preventive maintenance, and repair?

What allowance must be made for peak loads and schedules— when it is absolutely necessary to do the payroll, student registration, and next year's budget all on the same day?

Such questions must be answered at a rather grubby level of detail, and it is certainly not the president's problem to answer them all— or to know what the answers are. But the wise president assures himself that all such questions have been carefully considered and that the summary recommendations he receives represent the tip of a very large iceberg of facts.

When the requirements are finally understood, they can be translated into estimates of the size, speed, and complexity required in the hardware; estimates can then also be made of the personnel required to support the center. All these facts can then be translated into an estimated cost. If this turns out to be unrealistic or not feasible, the process must be iterated until requirements are satisfied. It should however be noted that, in many colleges, today's actual and accepted cost of services would have been considered totally unreasonable five years ago.

ACQUIRE PERSONNEL

Unless the college is fortunate enough to have people experienced in data processing, it will probably be necessary to hire at least one person whose primary and specific function will be in the area of computing. Ideally, this person should be hired early enough to take part in at least some of the work described above. Acquiring the right person for the job may take a long time; the process of searching for him should start as soon as the job can be defined. In addition, he should be employed as soon as he can be found, preferably well in advance of the delivery of hardware. He will be very busy with planning.

All institutions will find it useful to start working on this problem early; it may be one of the thorniest. Large private institutions, or those public ones which are relatively autonomous, are usually in the best position to retain competent personnel. Publicly supported institutions are often handicapped by civil service personnel and financial regulations that may seriously impede the development of effective systems. In one institution, part of a large state system, the computer center director told a sad and not untypical tale:

In our personnel system, there is no such classification as "program analyst," so I can't hire one openly. Instead, I have to hire him as a "maintenance mechanic, level III," and he's not happy about this on his employment record. The most I can pay a programmer is $360 a month! That's about the level of a junior clerk-typist. Those I do go out and get and train from the beginning leave me as soon as one of the local industrial firms finds out I have them. On the other hand, I have funds to go out and hire consultants and write subcontracts, with no regulations about pay. So I get around it by farming out the work, and the result is that it costs the taxpayer a lot more in the long run.

SELECT HARDWARE

If the committee does its job properly, the result will be a document describing in considerable detail the kinds of hardware needed and why. It should not be described in terms of specific trade-names: it is too easy to say, "Our college needs the ABC 123 computer." The committee states the requirements in terms of a range of size, speed, and input and output equipment, as well as required standard software. This description can then be submitted to various interested manufacturers for bids. The computer committee should also be responsible for helping to evaluate these bids (the lowest in price may not be the best) and recommend a computer system for the president's approval.

The detailed specifications should always include both present and anticipated requirements. For example, a system with four magnetic tape units may be needed now, but the manufacturer may be asked to provide a system which will eventually accommodate more as the system expands. A few years ago expanding a system often meant replacement of the central processor; any good *modern* system should now be upward-compatible (compatible with larger machines).

The committee may want to consider, if its requirements are modest, specifying that a *used* computer is acceptable or will be considered. It sometimes happens that a large system has replaced a smaller one in another institution, the latter or the manufacturer then being anxious to dispose of the earlier one. Many older computers, slower and/or smaller, can still be well worth their cost, especially to the smaller college. The college should beware, however, of a really obsolete computer. A lack of programs, service, and compatibility with others can make it not only a poor bargain, but actually a liability.

In some cases, it may be wise for the committee to submit part or all of their specifications in the form of described *applications* rather than in the technical format used to describe machines. For example, the specifications might read in part:

We need to process a file of 2,400 student records, each consisting of approximately 650 characters of information, six times a year, in serial order. Our personnel file, on which we would like to operate at random when it is being processed, contains approximately 400 characters for each of 180 employees. We expect both of these files to double in size within five years.

Or another example:

For experimental research in the physical sciences, we require a very high-speed processor, but the volume of data at input and output time is very small. Applications will include numerical integration, partial differential equations, complex numbers, etc. Direct input of digitalized data from a remote station should be possible within the next two years.

And so on.

As in the *estimating requirements* stage, it may be helpful for the committee to examine the specifications used by comparable institutions who have already been through this process. Some manufacturers may also be able to provide examples of such specifications from their own file.

In brief, the general table of contents for a set of specifications might read:

> Expected Administrative and Academic Applications
> Memory Size and Type (tape, disc, drum, core)
> Input/Output Units Needed
> Software and Support Requirements
> Maintenance Services Demanded
> Desired Delivery Date
> Expected or Projected Expansion Needs
> Acceptable Range of Cost
> Any Special Features (e.g., site preparation).

It may be possible that no one manufacturer can meet all of the specifications with any one machine. The specifications should be realistic, and the committee may have to be prepared to accept something less than perfect—either because of cost or because of unavailability of a particular combination of features.

DESIGN SYSTEMS

In estimating the requirements, assumptions were made about what the computer was to be used for. Now is the time to start tooling up. Decisions must be made as to what are the most crucial problems and what should be done in what order. Enough time must be allowed so that rash errors are not made. Automation seems to require much discipline of the people involved. Actually, what appears to be a need for more discipline is not related to the facts of automation but to the facts of change. Whenever people start doing things differently, they have to be much more careful and pay more attention to basic assumptions as well as to the details of particular processes.

The system designers will have to go to the users of information and find out what the people want and can use. Administrators must take the time to state what they are doing and what it is they want of the new system. The design of the system must be process-interactive; the system analyst must understand what it is the user wants, and the user must understand what it is the system can do for him. It is easy—and costly—to overestimate the speed with which all this can be accomplished.

It is very important, during this phase, for the president to bear in mind that *there is a temptation for line administrators to delegate to the system technicians much of their own essential responsibility to specify objectives.* It is perfectly proper to delegate responsibility for the "how" portions of a new process, but it is dangerous to delegate it for the "what." In the early stages, especially when the new technicalities seem forbidding, it is an easy temptation to think "I can never understand this, so I'll leave it to the programmer."

It should never be forgotten that whatever system emerges bears the same relation to the responsible administrator as did the earlier manual system being replaced. For example, any competent admissions officer understands the entire process by which applications are originated, reviewed, acted upon. If all or any portion of that system becomes computerized, the admissions officer must still understand every essential detail of its operation. There is nothing so complicated about computers and computerized systems that any administrator intelligent enough to understand his own existing system cannot master the required level of the new technology.

There is a temptation for many people to think of themselves as being nonmathematical or nonscientific and hence unable to comprehend the computer. One of the most difficult myths to dispel is that extensive mathematical background is required in the world of computing. Though the writing of scientific and mathematical programs requires understanding of the content, many administrative and information-processing technicians come from a wide variety of backgrounds, including the fine arts and humanities. The interest in *process*, and in symbolic processes especially, which so often underlies an interest in administration, is itself perhaps one of the few basic requirements for dealing with the computer.

ORIENTATION AND TRAINING

After the computer hardware has been ordered, and during the system design phase, it is not too early to begin planning and initiating a program of training and orientation so that all potential users of the computer center can prepare to take advantage of its services. If courses or workshops are to be presented as soon as the equipment is installed and operating, lead time will have to be provided for course development. Those involved in helping specify their needs for the system designers and developers will of course begin their orientation almost immediately. In fact, learning how to explain what they need and learning what the system can do for them turns out to have considerable instructional value.

Some machine manufacturers provide training courses for customers. Some of these are taught on the campus or at nearby facilities where demonstration equipment is already available. In some cases, seminars and workshops for administrators are held at the manufacturer's classrooms, sometimes at a comfortable lodge or retreat. This permits the administrator to get away from the office for a few days and, free of interruptions, concentrate on the problem of learning to understand his new resources.

The top level of the administration, including the president, needs to have enough information about computer characteristics and capabilities (*not* operations or programming) in order to make appropriate decisions and requests for service. One of the best ways to gain rapid insight into these matters is to study examples of the results of systems already in existence at other institutions. Most machine vendors can supply such examples. It is often useful to invite the director of another college's information system or computer center to visit the campus (perhaps as a paid consultant) and bring examples of his work, together with the explanatory documents he has developed for his own users. If it is practical to do so, such a sharing of information might be done on the campus of the institution being used as an example.

Those clerical and technical personnel who will not be part of the center staff but whose work will involve liaison with the center should be provided with sufficient training and orientation to ensure smooth functioning of the new system. (During this phase, it often happens that the clerical staff and administrative aides make useful suggestions about features of the new system as they learn what the equipment can do.)

The next large group which will require orientation and assistance, if not indeed some training in programming, is the faculty. Those in the hard sciences may already have some background, but they may need assistance in learning how to use the new or upgraded facilities. It is unsafe to generalize too glibly, but today's programming languages can be learned, with average effort, in a few days or weeks. Five two-hour lecture sessions, with homework assignments and some opportunity to write and run simple programs, are sufficient to get the faculty started. (At one college, the first course in programming was taught to faculty members by a junior student who had mastered it at a nearby college.) Most vendors who supply good software also supply good reference manuals, and many faculty members observe that after they once get the hang of problem-oriented programming languages (FORTRAN, COBOL, ALGOL), the best way to learn effective programming is to tackle some familiar problems. The reference manuals are extremely useful, as they provide sample solutions and clear explanations.

In addition to general orientation courses or sessions, it is helpful in larger institutions to provide some courses which are specifically directed to a given field. For example, the kinds of sample problems that would be appropriate for engineers or physicists would be quite different from those provided for psychologists or historians. The former would profit by studying examples of techniques for handling advanced mathematical techniques, while the latter would be more interested in handling nonnumeric information, the analysis of statistical data, and perhaps content analysis, abstracting, or bibliographic techniques.

Finally there is the student. It has been observed on many campuses that students seem to soak up computing techniques almost by osmosis or as part of the student folk-culture, but this is not necessarily efficient or effective. At a growing number of colleges, competence in computer programming is demanded of all or most first-year students, and those entering freshmen who cannot already demonstrate such competence (an increasing number of high schools are now teaching programming) are asked to take either a regular full-semester course or an intensive workshop. As an alternative or supplement to course work, there are several excellent self-instructional texts from which any reasonably diligent student (or faculty member) can learn the essentials of even the most up-to-date programming techniques. The fact that most students bright enought to survive their freshman year of college can master programming by the end of it should be encouraging to the faculty.

ATTITUDINAL PROBLEMS

Sometimes things can go wrong! Despite every care, something doesn't work quite right, and everyone seems to be complaining loudly and wildly about the dangers of automation and depersonalization. News media delight in picking up these stories of how "the computer goofed again." These cases are far from unusual:

The faculty rejects the new student information system and the computer processing of grades because it excessively standardizes their grading procedures.

The students rebel at automated and depersonalized procedures; they deliberately fold, spindle, or mutilate.

The administrative staff feels they are being replaced and that brash young upstarts are trying to redesign a system that they have spent decades perfecting.

After careful planning, getting the right machine, a workable schedule, and a working program, the whole thing seems to blow up and the decision-makers feel they have made some terrible blunder. What went wrong?

Staff Attitudes

People like the status quo and do not like to see the known replaced by the unknown, especially if they fear that there may not be a place for them in a new system. Wasserman expresses this problem as it occurs in libraries:

Certain large organizations which have a record of stability . . . tend to be staffed by individuals with lower tolerance for accepting radical change than those in organizations more vulnerable to competition, cyclical employment, variations, and lesser security of employment. Mechanization advances the acceleration of the formalization of the organization, resulting in a furthering of the rationalization of work brought about through the substitution of rules for judgment, and leading to a reduction in the number of status posts and a higher degree of centralized administration.[1]

College administrators and the staffs that work for them are likely to be very conservative in their attitudes toward change. Especially in the lower ranks this may take the form of heel dragging rather than outright opposition. When the system seriously falters, however, some of this opposition may come into the open, fists clenched. The advent of the new system must be explained exhaustively, carefully, and repeatedly to everyone concerned. It should be seen as an opportunity to do jobs faster and better; never as a challenge to competency or job security.

Sometimes a system failure of the kind here being discussed can be traced to a lack of proper cooperation between the system technicians and the system users in the design phase. If the understanding is that the technicians are designing a system, the users do not consider themselves involved and feel it is up to the technicians to make the system work. If the technicians make it plain, however, that the users themselves must take a vital role in the design of the system, they will also take a vital interest in seeing that it does the job that needs to be done—and does it well.

The administrator must ultimately think of it as "our" system—not "theirs" (the center's). In a student information system, for example, it is the registrar's responsibility to see that the system suits the needs of the college and allows him to perform his job in the way he understands it needs to be done. If he abrogates this responsibility, and lays it upon a technician who knows about computers but not

[1] Paul Wasserman, *The Librarian and the Machine* (Detroit: Gale Research Co., 1965), p. 30.

about registration at this college, the chances of success are diminished.

Ignorance of computers or systems of the future is bound to create some fear and hostility. Knowledge of what computers can do if they are properly used seems to result in improved interest and enthusiasm.

Student Attitudes

The most commonly observed adverse reactions to automation are found among students. They rebel at what seems to them a growing wave of standardization, depersonalization, and regimentation. The automated system and the punched card with a number instead of a name are symbols of this tendency in our society. They react strongly to the symbol, more because of their general feelings about automation than because of a specific complaint about the system.

Their fears are not without some justification. Every citizen encounters many automated systems—at his bank, at the telephone, in his charge accounts, in his dealings with any large organization. Many of these encounters are with systems less satisfactory to him than the earlier manual systems. It appears to him that all automated systems (or at least the great majority) were designed to make machines happy regardless of the inconvenience to people, and this is unfortunately sometimes true. But the fault is not with the punched card or with the computer. It is with the technician who designed the system to optimize the machine aspects at the expense of the human aspects—and it is with the administrator who lets this happen.

If the student is treated impersonally, and if registration is more difficult, confusing, and time-consuming than it used to be, *the fault is not with the computer* or with automation in general. *It is precisely where it has always been—with the system's human designers.* A good automated student record system, as has been pointed out many times, enhances rather than decreases individual attention to students. Rourke and Brooks point out:

> Registrars and admissions officers . . . commonly argue that use of the computer makes it possible to deal with the student on a personal basis by freeing administrators from the burden of clerical chores that would otherwise consume an increasing proportion of their time in the face of expanding enrollments and the increased range and complexity of university course offerings . . . .
>
> It can be also contended, although admissions officers did not usually argue this way, that the computer itself has certain characteristics such as speed and versatility in operation, not to mention unlimited patience, that enable it in certain areas to give each student a degree of personal concern that no system of human administration would today find feasible on a large campus.[2]

As with the administrative staff which is to be involved in the use of the system, students too must be kept informed and allowed to advise in the development of the system. At one college, a representative of the student council was a member of the design group working on student records. Before the system is installed, students should understand what it is to be, why it is being instituted, and (most important) how it is to help them.

Once students learn to deal with the automated system and see it for what it is, rather than as a symbol, they will usually find it quite acceptable and as interesting to deal with as the system it replaces—

---

[2] Rourke and Brooks, "The 'Managerial Revolution' in Higher Education," *Administrative Science Quarterly*, September 1964, p. 171.

perhaps more so. At one university which has an automated scheduling program, the scheduling officer was asked about student attitudes. It seemed to the interviewer that manual scheduling systems were considered a fine challenge to the student—to avoid early morning, Friday afternoon, or Saturday classes, for example. Hadn't some of the sport gone out of registration? On the contrary, he replied. The game to beat the computer is a lively game indeed, with several sophisticated techniques. The fact that it is automated means only that it is consistent, patient, and subject to trickery. There is room still for initiative in registration.

MAKING SURE

There are four important rules for avoiding the trap of adverse reaction: *education, involvement, safeguards,* and *patience.*

The impact community must be educated as to the reasons for the new system and what its advantages will be, for the community as a whole, and for the individual segments of the community which will deal most closely with the system. Most people who are opposed to the idea of automation are opposed out of ignorance—or as a result of an unfortunate experience with bad systems.

All those who will be in a position to complain effectively later should be involved in the design. Their advice should be sought and their reactions to proposed innovations listened to carefully. It is their requirements that the system will have to satisfy; it is best to find out what those requirements are before the system is built.

Safeguards are enormously important. An accident on the first day the system is unveiled may ruin its usefulness forever; the future of automation on the campus in any form may be postponed a number of years. Especially if the system is the first one, or is a very visible one (like registration), ample time should be allowed for exhaustive testing. One college president wrote:

We cannot afford an accident that would be embarrassing to the data processing system. If you have one, I am afraid that you will never recover from the psychological effect. You will be condemned forever.[3]

Finally, some patience is required. No system was ever designed which did not have some bugs left in it or that did not annoy some-

[3] Jack R. Woolf in *Proceedings of the Ninth College and University Machine Records Conference* (Palo Alto, Calif.: Educational Systems Corp., 1964), p. 9.

one. Stereotypes die hard, and it will take the new system time to prove itself to its users.

It is important to note that the president may have to protect the system and its designers from warranted but short-sighted criticism when things go wrong in shake-down phases of development. One computer center director was asked by his president if there was any way in which he could help. "Yes, sir," he was told. "Have faith!"

8

ORGANIZING COMPUTER SERVICES

THE ADMINISTRATOR soon discovers that computers are expensive. Even as a gift, it is voracious in its requirements for supplies, maintenance, and high-priced manpower. If it is used successfully, people are already talking about replacing it with a bigger and more expensive one. Many a college president feels he is riding the tiger: he cannot get off, and he does not know where it is taking him. In such a position, he may become aware that the computer center requires management in a stricter sense than do most other kinds of college facilities.

Most college administrators shy away from the sound and implications of the word "management," especially with regard to anything the faculty takes an interest in, but the imperatives must be faced squarely. The president's haunting fear that his computer facilities are not being used with maximum effectiveness is probably well founded; understanding how computer resources are being spent, and how they can be controlled, however, requires sound management practices, no matter how the word makes the academician wince.

"Managing" the computer center may be resisted by the users because they fear this will restrict what they can do. However, if an institution thinks it is valuable, for example, to let students run their own programs, even if they do it inefficiently, the open shop should be permitted—but knowingly. There is nothing wrong with facing up to what this part of a student's (or faculty member's) education costs.

There is another reason for wanting to see the computer center well managed. Its presence on the campus affects a great many people in different ways; it is rarely a matter of indifference. There may be intense rivalries for its control; complaints and misunderstandings can damage the effectiveness not only of the computer center but of the college as a whole. *The president must assure himself that the center is being run fairly for all parties concerned and is not being used as a pawn in some power struggle.*

When computers were new to the campus, they were at first treated as pieces of laboratory equipment—as indeed they were. However, when some of the broad range of uses of computers began to be understood, and as interest in these machines spread beyond engineers and scientists, people began to see in them a broadly useful resource. The analogy to the library is often cited in this context, and sometimes this has been very helpful. (The reader will find the analogy drawn at several points in this book.) But now that this analogy is becoming a truism, it may be wise to remind people again that the computer *is*, after all, a piece of laboratory equipment (albeit in a very new kind of laboratory) and is *different from a library in many important ways.* Computers are in important ways different from any other facility or device with which the college has to deal. Analogies may be useful in some instances, but ultimately the computer must be dealt with on its own terms. Policies for its use must be decided on the basis of new criteria.

There are a few very simple rules that can be drawn from the experience of successful managers of computer centers:

The individual who has primary responsibility for the center must be highly knowledgeable and respected for his technical ability by all users; yet he must be able to discuss computer problems with both faculty and administration *in their terms.*

The computer center should be placed in the organization so as to be accessible to all users and potential users. Any hint of bias or influence will hamper its usefulness.

The centralization of computing facilities presents a great opportunity for economy—but a challenge to effective management.

This chapter will attempt to expand these three principles. To simplify the exposition, we shall consider the case of the college that has a computer system which meets the requirements of administration, research, and instruction. There may be more than a single machine. They may even be in several locations. They are nevertheless all part of a single *system* or organization in the administrative structure.

ORGANIZATION

The operation of the computer center must be the responsibility of a single individual who desires to run it to the satisfaction of the users—the administration and the academic community. Broader responsibility (such as policy decisions) may be vested in a policy committee and/or a user's group, but the day-to-day interpretation of policy in terms of specific problems must be done quickly. This can only be done by an experienced individual.

At one small college, a committee acts as center director, and the result is chaos. Users with problems approach members of the committee for problem resolution, only to receive ambiguous and contradictory advice. The result is that the computer *operators* control the installation. Potential users are so intimidated or confused that they either go off campus for their computer needs or avoid the use of the computer altogether.

Even a small college can rarely afford *not* to employ a *full-time* director. If he shares his time between the computer center and an academic appointment, one post or the other will suffer. If his true interest is his teaching and research, he will run the center with his left hand, and eventually the center will be left to run itself. It is usually true that an organization that runs itself runs down.

The director must supply a broad range of services. Besides the mechanics of keeping the center running, he will be a real force, encouraging new and useful applications and guiding the novice. One state university developed detailed specifications for what they expected from their computer center director. One of the major ones is worth quoting at length:

He shall be responsible to give leadership to the development and application of the university's information processing capabilities by:

advising and consulting with *all* segments of the university on information processing problems and potentialities;

assisting with the development of research proposals that involve information processing;

fostering research and development of new applications and technologies, especially those of potential interest and value to the university;

maintaining an awareness of the current state-of-the-art in the information processing field;

promoting and assisting in the development, within the academic departments, of necessary computer courses at all levels.

It is not surprising that such posts frequently stand open for long periods of time, even at very attractive salaries. The potential computing center director must have considerable experience in information processing, a talent for politics and human management, the academic background to discuss research intelligently with faculty users, and a thorough understanding of college administrative operations. He is not easy to find.

If the computer center is to be a central service, it should not fall under the control of a single interest group, or its value to other users will be lessened. In this case, the analogy of the library is a good one. John Hamblen writes:

The head of the Information Processing Center should report to the top administrative official equal to or higher than that of any of the divisions which the center serves. In most institutions this implies that the head of the center reports to the President or Executive Vice President.[1]

In many colleges, the center director reports to the dean of the college or academic vice-president. If the function of the center is totally academic, this allows him to deal with all the departments in an unbiased manner. It will not, however, induce the administrative users to entrust him with their problems. At another college, the computer was first acquired for administrative use and is part of the comptroller's organization. Faculty users feel they receive second-class treatment—yet the comptroller cannot understand why they want a machine of their own.

The director needs the political neutrality he can get only by reporting to the office of the president. And he needs the influence and leverage which the support of the president can give him, if he is to balance inevitably conflicting forces and interests. The term "office of the president" should not be strictly interpreted to mean the president himself. In large or rapidly growing institutions, the president may be far too busy to give the computer center director necessary support and leadership. Assignment of responsibility to an executive (or administrative) vice-president may have the same effect. How-

[1] John Hamblen, "Coordination of Administrative, Research, and Instructional Uses of Data Processing Equipment in Colleges and Universities," ICC Bulletin, April 1964, p. 90.

ever, in moments of real crisis, the president himself should be prepared to devote his attention to the settlement of vital issues and lend his authority to resulting decisions.

Other than assuring neutrality, top administration has another service it must provide the computer center director: the arbitration of disputes over the allocation of resources. The problems of resource allocation may become particularly acute while the system is in the development and implementation stages. One data processing manager complains:

There are many projects we are obliged to spend resources on—more than we can handle. I don't have the authority or the facts to determine priorities. I need someone to tell me the relative importance of each of these demands.

POLICY DETERMINATION

The highly placed and sheltered computer center director need not be an autocrat; nor must he expect the college president to determine all policy for him. He needs and should expect the help of a college-wide policy committee. Some directors are astute enough to run the operation as benevolent despots, but it takes an unusual sensitivity and political sense to be able to establish and modify policy in such a way as to keep all of the conflicting forces happily at bay. The more usual director will be grateful for the help of a committee. If it performs no other function, it serves as an arena in which to review and resolve conflicts. It allows top administration to keep from becoming involved in technical details and allows the faculty to maintain some sort of titular control.

Use of Committees

Such committees will usually have representatives from each using department (or group of departments, where the use is slight, as in the humanities) and from the administration. If, for example, the committee is to determine policies with regard to fiscal matters (charging for time, acquiring new equipment), there should be a representative of the college's business office. It is important, however, that each user have a clear line of communication to this committee: students through faculty advisors to a specific committee member. Thus no user is ever frustrated from presenting his complaints and suggestions.

Such committees have worked in various ways at different colleges, according to the size of the college, the sophistication of the users, and the personalities involved. In one small college, the committee rarely meets. When the director has a problem, he calls the committee chairman, who either makes a decision on the spot or calls one or two key members. At one state university, the computer center director viewed the committee as a bother, "They occasionally give me gratuitous advice, but it has never come to blows."

One small but sophisticated institution has in fact *two* committees. One, responsible for broad policy, is chaired by a vice-president and contains division chairmen and several key members of the administration. Another committee consists of faculty only and speaks for the users; their discussions are more technically oriented.

Another comparable institution—small but sophisticated in the use of computers—has no committee. It may serve as an example of the dangers of not supplying adequate lines of communication. The director of the center explained to a visitor that there was no need for a committee: all of the users were satisfied, and he himself kept top administration informed of what was going on. The visitor heard the same report from the administration. It did not take him many hours, however, to learn that the service was so bad that many faculty members were going off campus to get their requirements satisfied. Since there is no formal communication mechanism, and since the computer center director has the president's ear, they do not even bother to complain. They find ways to do their work without involving the center.

Again the library provides a useful but not exact analogy. One computer center director put it this way:

Every faculty department and school has a library committee. They get so-and-so much money, and they decide what to request the librarian to obtain for them. They wouldn't think of shrugging off this responsibility. Until we have faculty committees which are interested in—and take responsibility for—the allocation of computer resources, the computer will remain a foreign body in this institution.

Another director said:

It just takes time. Wait until the new generation of graduate students hits the faculty deck. They won't be satisfied with anything less than the best. Wait another generation, and we won't have these lonely uphill battles against faculty indifference.

ACADEMIC AND ADMINISTRATIVE CONFLICT

Sooner or later the college will face the issue of centralization or decentralization, or of having one large machine versus several small ones. The issue is most likely to arise in the natural bifurcation between academic and administrative interests and uses.

Many faculty members will eventually use the college's computer in their research. Most students will learn to use it and to solve some classroom and textbook problems. The administration will use it for routine and repetitive clerical tasks, to create and analyze new information about the college and its functions, and to help make decisions about present and future problems. As usage increases and the supply of unused or idle time on the machine begins to dwindle, there are conflicts of demand.

Among *academic* users there is often some conflict and competition, but they are basically the same kind of users and share common problems and a common attitude. The various *administrative* departments using the computer will occasionally be in conflict but will have a basic community of interest sufficient to work these problems out. Between academic and administrative users, however, there sometimes arise conflicts which are not easily resolved unless great care is taken to protect the interests of both. The alternative is for the college to support two or more computer centers. A great many do now.

Symptoms of such conflict are not hard to find. At one small college, the registrar is using a computer center designed primarily for the scientific or academic user. The registrar's information on disc files has been accidentally erased several times. The data can be reconstructed; it is more insult than injury. It appears to the registrar that the center staff does not take his work seriously. The academician likes to see a center run in a free and easy manner; the administrator prefers a more business-like operation.

At colleges where computer sciences are taught, the system of operation of the center itself is considered an object of research and is subject to frequent and sometimes confusing modification. The result may be an unstable system of operation. To the administrative user such a way of operation is simply intolerable—or at best unreliable and expensive.

Academic people who run computer centers are indeed sometimes unfair to the administrative user. When the machine is new and there is considerable idle time, they are anxious to have new users and may solicit the business of the administrative officers, who tend to develop straightforward, predictable usage patterns. Later however, when computer time begins to be at a premium, the administrative user may find that he is no longer welcome. In this case he is certainly justified in thinking he has been misled.

In all fairness, it must be mentioned that the academician can also feel himself slighted. At one institution, a visitor was confidentially informed by administrators that the academic users were always given priority and by members of the computer science department that the administrators were always given priority. It appeared to be a company with two prima donnas.

Although the split between academic and administrative users is most common, further divisions are also possible—even likely if natural growth is allowed to grow unchecked and uncontrolled. Unable to get the services he feels he requires many a user will try to convince the administration that he needs his own machine; not a few of them will be successful. At one institution the administrative functions centering around fiscal affairs use the comptroller's computer; those centering around student records use the computer housed in the office of institutional studies. At another college, data processing was centralized until a prominent scientist on the faculty was able to fund his own machine from a research contract. He began to operate his own center, and other scientists were encouraged to do the same.

Grosch's Law

Early in the history of computers, Herbert Grosch formulated the general rule-of-thumb that the capability of computers varies as the square of their price. Thus a given unit of computation is cheaper to perform on a large machine than on a small one. In a field subject to frequent revolutionary upheaval, this rule has remained remarkably accurate. The price of computation for all sizes of machines has fallen dramatically in the past ten years; yet it is still true that it is cheaper to perform most work on one large machine than on two small ones.

And a Corollary

Some unknown management scientist, faced with the seemingly irrefutable argument of Grosch's law, soon phrased the corollary: *The advantages of centralization are seen by users as accruing to management; the disadvantages to the rank and file.* Management can enforce centralization in order to realize the economic benefits, but the users face the problems of scheduling, allocating resources, and the sheer inconvenience of wanting to use the machine when it is tied up with someone else's work.

There are advantages to centralization other than the cost of computing. Less capacity is required to meet peak loads; operating and maintenance costs are less; and some programs can be run on a large machine which cannot be run on two small ones. These advantages accrue to the college as a whole; the last one particularly will interest users, but it is not an economic consideration.

Buffering and Priorities

On the other hand, from the point of view of the user there are serious problems in centralization; it is he, after all, who faces the problem of a computer center preoccupied with the work of some other user. If the centralized system is to succeed, some mechanism must exist to buffer the various user groups from one another. This can be accomplished by assigning percentages of available resources to user groups, who can then suballocate among themselves. The administrative and academic users, for example, are each assigned a part of the available computing power; they need not encroach on one another's access and can avoid conflict.

If experience with usage rates is used to establish allocations, then the whole rationing mechanism may be periodically readjusted to changing patterns of use. During uncongested periods (hopefully most of the time), no rationing will be required, and hence usage rates will be free to change. Such an allocation scheme is not based on priorities.

The main function of a priority system is to adjust the probability of meeting job completion deadlines. Priority mechanisms allow some users to get better service than others, *but the victory is hollow if all service is poor.* Moreover, such rules invariably break down in the face of congestion: too many users get into the "top priority" class, while other classes get no service at all.

Other Resource Allocation Problems

The rationing-buffering problem affects all user groups in a uniform way. Other allocation problems generated by centralized computer facilities are more selective. Some users may tend to believe that rank has its privileges; consequently they will often resist any policy that prevents invoking priority due to rank. Undergraduate students are generally of lowest rank and thus are in position to be given short shrift whenever congestion occurs. Instructors of undergraduate courses will be affected and can invoke their rank, but eventually the pecking order asserts itself: there is more and more "top priority" work.

The solution seems to be a policy of allocation and not of priority. Each user or user group can subdivide his allotment on the basis of his own estimate of the relative importance of each individual job without disturbing the whole system. Such allocation must include provision for undergraduate courses, homework, and student projects.

Most funded research projects will not present special problems. However, occasionally some project will have needs which cannot be met without causing undue disruption of the normal operation of a central service. In this case, there is justification for a separate center or machine installation. This justification is based on a need to innovate without disrupting the public-utility-like services of the computing facility. Decentralization of facilities can still, however, be accompanied by centralized management. Given a policy of centralization of management and a policy of trying to centralize the allocation of facilities as appropriate, the problem of dedicating specific hardware facilities to specific users can be dealt with in the following framework:

If funds are available to support a separate dedicated hardware system and these funds cannot be channeled into the central facility budget, then the separate facility should probably be approved. This does not automatically imply that the separate, dedicated equipment should be separately housed or separately administered.

If funds are available to one user and can be channeled into the central facility budget, then the equipment in question should be integrated into the central facility with the understanding that the user who brought in the funds should have first claim.

There should be few calls for dedication of specific facilities to users to be supported by university funds. This means that any such call for dedication must be adequately justified and perhaps separately funded.

INTERINSTITUTIONAL COOPERATION

In the interviews which formed the basis of this report, a topic of widespread interest was intercollege sharing of computers. For many small colleges any computer at all is a considerable expense; a computer large enough to support faculty research projects of any magnitude may appear out of the question. Given the concept of time-sharing and the arguments for centralization the appeal of the cooperative computer center is obvious. Any plan for multi-institutional cooperative ventures, however, must be devised with caution. Smaller colleges, to whom such a plan is most likely to appeal, are also the colleges who are most concerned about their autonomy and the maintenance of their own individuality. Yet in sharing a common facility for the good of all the members, some autonomy and control must be relinquished.

A cooperative venture may take several forms. The ideal that comes immediately to mind is a time-shared system of sufficient size and complexity, with on-line terminals located throughout the campuses of all the participating colleges. But less ambitious plans are also possible—perhaps more possible. A smaller center, operated in the batch-processing mode, might be located so that a courier service could provide fast and convenient service to all the members. The most successful cooperative ventures have been centered around a large university which could provide service to a number of local colleges. It is interesting to note, however, the usual result of this form of symbiosis: the small college learns the value of computing by using the university center and ends by trying to justify a computer of its own.

Possible Disadvantages

There are four principal disadvantages of a computer shared among equals (as opposed to a large university sharing with small colleges): (1) inconvenient geography, (2) loss of autonomy and control, (3) financial risk, and (4) difficulty of projection and planning.

If the computer is to be shared, it cannot be located on every campus. It will be on one or in a separate location. This means that all users cannot gain equally easy access to it. It also means that it is not a part of the campus which can be shown off to visiting firemen. This may seem a trivial point, but in many colleges it is an important one. In a small private college, it may be easier to find a donor to give the college a computer of its own than to raise the funds to support a fraction of a computer center located in some neutral territory. The only argument against these points is reason. It is not the glittering lights and the shining machinery that lend a college distinction but the work that can in fact be accomplished.

The loss of autonomy and control can seem a very real threat. If there is a conflict among the users (as there is bound to be as soon as computer use begins to exceed available capacity), someone must resolve the difficulty by refusing to allow some users as much computer time as they ask for. The authority for such decisions must be exercised by an independent computer center director, in accord with the policies of the intercollege committee. Once this authority is delegated, the college must adhere to it, no matter who is offended, but unhappiness may still be expressed—ultimately perhaps as secession.

There is some financial risk involved in a center to be shared among equals. For if each college puts into the common fund as much as it can sensibly and profitably spend on computers, all are committed as far as they reasonably can be. If one of the members, due to poor planning or lack of agreement on policies withdraws from the agreement, the others must absorb the additional expense or drop the whole idea. Either of these alternatives must be unpalatable or unworkable.

Estimates for the Future

If the cooperative center is well planned and begins operation, there are still future problems. As computer usage grows, estimates of future use and plans and budgets for future developments must be made. This means that all of the colleges must plan along compatible lines and in compatible terms. They may begin to feel again that they are losing their autonomy and being forced to produce a coordinated plan in education, in research, in administration. Their data processing plans involve all of these.

These difficulties can be overcome if the institutions involved are willing to live with the inconveniences in order to reap the benefits. The Southern Regional Education Board has published an extremely useful booklet on the subject.[2] This paper concludes with a set of several recommendations for groups interested in looking into the feasibility of cooperation in this area. Some of them are cited here, by way of conclusion.

Interinstitutional cooperation and coordination is becoming extremely attractive, particularly between a large university and its neighboring small colleges or among institutions within a given higher education system.

Highly competent planning groups are required for interinstitutional cooperation. The operating function can either be delegated to one institution or to a nonprofit corporation. . . .

Collectively the planning group should be well-informed about patterns, purposes, and costs of computer education and associated computer costs. They should be able to differentiate between the characteristics of different types of education programs. . . . They should be aware of the different requirements for research, instruction, administration, and area service use of computers.

The group should formulate a plan, and take steps continuously to motivate,

[2] John Hamblen and William F. Atchison, *Cooperative Planning for Computers and Computer Science Programs in Higher Education* (Atlanta: Southern Regional Education Board, 1966).

evaluate, and revise the plan so that the computing needs of higher education will continue to be met in the most effective manner.

The recommendations of the planning group should be compatible with the funds available for implementation.

On the last point: *Amen.*

OPERATING THE COMPUTER CENTER

THE COMPUTER CENTER DIRECTOR and his policy advisory committee have three primary questions to answer:

What services will the center provide?

What staff is needed to supply these services?

What costing policies will be applied?

These questions will be examined briefly here.

ACCESSIBILITY AND SERVICES

It may be thought to be obvious what services the center will provide: the computer center offers the user access to the machine; the role of the center staff is to expedite this access and to prevent new or incompetent users from damaging anything. This is of course true, but it is also somewhat naive. At a number of colleges which had no computer or had just acquired one, the faculty and staff were asked what they needed. The attitudes of many were reflected in the remark of a professor of economics: "The lack of a competent staff is much more inhibiting than the lack of a computer. I've always been able to find a computer I could use somewhere, but it's harder to get competent advice and help."

The novice user will want help with his programming; even the more sophisticated user will want some consulting services in formulating problems. Unless the user is himself an expert in information processing technology, he will probably be able to make use of some service other than having someone open the computer room for business each morning.

What services will the center and its staff provide? The answer depends primarily on three variables: (1) the size (and budget) of the center; (2) the sophistication of the average user; and (3) the history of computing on campus. If the computer is a small one, and if the budget is limited, there will not be a large staff. In this case, little can be offered beyond access to the machine and an opportunity for the user to solve his own problems by trial and error. On the other hand, if the center has a large and expensive machine, economy will necessitate a staff adequate to assure that the machine is used efficiently and effectively.

A few examples may illustrate the range of possibilities. The following pattern is common to many colleges with a small computer. Prospective users take a programming course given by a part-time director. Once they have demonstrated their competence to operate the machine, they are given a key to the computer room. If they have problems they consult the director, but they are more likely to turn to one another.

Some faculty to whom the computer is new will at first enjoy doing their own programming. It is a new experience, and the actual process of writing and checking out programs gives users useful insights into the nature of the process. They will eventually, however, decide that they know enough about it and will prefer to use professional programmers. (It may be possible to find graduate students or faculty wives to do this.) On the other hand, they may prefer that the regular computing center staff provide such service.

If there is large use in a particular area (say statistics), faculty members will want a professional competent in this area to whom they can turn with their problems. This is likely to be the computer center director himself. For one thing, the director will probably know what programs are already available at other institutions or from cooperative *user groups* (informal leagues among computer users with common interests). The director can also help faculty groups with common general problems develop libraries and packages of programs. At one university for example, there is a magnetic tape library of programs commonly used by statisticians. The user brings in his data and places a calling card at the beginning of it which calls forth a complete program for correlations, factor analysis, and multivariate treatment.

Such conveniences exist where the director has exhibited that *concern for the user's welfare* which must be his outstanding characteristic and which makes him worth so much to the college.

Administrative users are liable to be less patient than faculty with mere access to the computer. They will expect the center to provide them with system analysis and programming support. They may require the more far-ranging advice of a management consultant in the design of systems.

One of the first additional services the center will consider as usage approaches the limit of available time.is the help of a computer operator. When everyone has a key and operates his own program, the user who finds the center busy must either wait or come back later. Having an operating staff enables him to deliver his job to the computer and pick it up after it has been run. The experienced computer user will thus be relieved of an onerous chore; his time, he knows, is better spent at the considerable intellectual labors that computer use entails than in processing his own work. However, users with less experience are liable to be less pleased. When one is only beginning to use a computer, there is a surprising amount of satisfaction in operating the machine and watching one's job being processed. Students in particular feel strongly that direct contact with the machine is an important part of their education. They are very likely to be mistaken, however. Their interest in a mysterious and fabulously expensive computer is analogous to their interest in (say) high-performance automobiles. A motto prominently displayed in one college computer center is worth noting: THE OBJECT OF COMPUTING IS INSIGHT, NOT NUMBERS.

User Training

An important key to accessibility is internal training of users. Many potential users of a computer are put off because they do not know how to get started or are afraid of doing the wrong thing and hence wasting their time and effort. Although particularly true of administrative personnel, it is true of the faculty at many colleges as well. Leaving aside the question of the training of students, there are three areas where training may be needed:

Top administration must learn to ask the right questions.

The administrative community must learn what things are possible and economical and how to achieve them.

The faculty must learn how this new tool can help them with some of their old problems.

Part of the education of administrators, faculty, and staff is to learn what the computer is and can do. This training often includes a course (sometimes very elementary) in programming. Even though the student may never plan to do any programming himself, such study is often the easiest way to understand the potentialities of data processing. Some of the mystery of the machine disappears when an individual learns how easy it is to direct and control it.

Another important function of educating potential users is to excite their imagination by the ways in which computers can be useful in their own work. Most administrators and some faculty will see obvious applications, such as doing tedious clerical chores presently done by hand. But many of the most significant possible uses of the computer can be found only by thinking in much broader terms, by reevaluating present methods. In research for example, it may be obvious that tabulation and statistical correlation of experimental results can be done by computers. It is more difficult to realize how a reexamination of the goals of the research may lead to a fruitful use of the computer in the design and conduct of the experiments themselves. Examples in administration are easy to find. There are a hundred colleges using the computer merely to compute the payroll for each college using it as an aid in sophisticated budgeting, planning, or decision-making.

Education in seeing such wide-ranging possibilities can be encouraged in several ways. A skillful computer center director will encourage those who bring him problems to view those problems in the broadest terms. He will in fact encourage them to bring him their *problems*, not their preplanned solutions. In this way a computer-based solution, taking full advantage of the potentialities (and economies) of the computer, is more likely to be reached.

In order to guarantee that faculty and administration use computers well, it is crucial that key users and potential users of computer services consult colleagues who have been using a computer. Nothing can convince a registrar, a librarian, or a linguist of the potentials of the computer nearly so well as conversation with another registrar, librarian, or linguist. Scientists are more likely to be aware of computer applications, but administrators may need to visit other institutions to learn what it is possible to do.

Many scholars and administrators will feel that this new technology is beyond them, that it is for the younger generation to implement computer-based systems. One cannot force esteemed scholars to reevaluate their methods, or registrars or deans to investigate new techniques of administration. But they should certainly be given every opportunity to learn what their colleagues are doing. It will surprise them to learn how simple some applications really are.

User's Handbook

In many colleges and universities with successful service centers, there is often a user's handbook describing both objectives and means of attainment. The creation of such a handbook is a useful exercise: it compels everyone to be explicit about goals. The college will find it helpful to obtain examples of such handbooks from other institutions if a model is not at hand. (Most large universities, or those with long-established centers, are able to supply such manuals.) The general nature of the problems which the computer center staff must ultimately think through may perhaps be conveyed by describing the contents of a typical manual intended for the center's users:

Introduction: the history and general objectives of providing computer facilities.

Facilities: this section lists the names (manufacturer and model number) of all the college's computers, and their geographical location, and lists the auxiliary equipment (keypunches, sorters, tabulators, etc.) which students and faculty may use. If plans are firm for obtaining new equipment, users are often interested to know what can be expected and when so that they can think ahead to new applications; this should be included.

Rules and regulations: there should be detailed description of such items as:

Procedures for establishing an account at the center.

Regular hours of operation of all facilities available to persons other than the center's staff.

Hours at which various kinds of computer runs are made (for example, production runs, program check-out, one-hour turn-around for short programs or subroutines, instruction in machine operations).

Hours when programmers and consultants are available and where.

Hourly (or other) charges for computer time and use of auxiliary equipment.

Requirements for computer program documentation.

Software resources: this section describes the programming languages (assemblers, compilers) available for each computer and may also indicate what courses are taught for each. It may describe the general-purpose programs available from the center's library, with procedures for obtaining and using them, and a description of the center's reference library.

Instructions: some manuals contain detailed explanations, with examples, of how to prepare input materials (programs, data) for the various software systems. If time-shared remote terminals are available, there are instructions for getting into and out of the system. (Some centers provide make-ready space for students to use in assembling materials and inspecting output, and in larger centers arrangements are made for students to store materials in card file drawers or cubbyholes.)

Do's and don't's: the accumulated folklore of the center is sometimes summarized in a short section which tells the user what to do to avoid trouble and how to diagnose common difficulties. If there are time periods when various kinds of equipment are not in great demand, it may be suggested that users can avoid queuing or waiting at such hours.

Miscellany: some manuals provide a bibliography of reference materials, self-instructional manuals for programming systems, recommended readings, etc. Others may even list examples of typical applications in various fields, especially when the newcomer may not be aware of all the possibilities. One college manual lists the names of specialists in various departments who have had experience with applications in their own academic fields.

Addenda: more elaborate manuals show the floor plan of the center, list the center personnel, provide examples of flow charts and rules for drawing them, and make additional suggestions about related facilities (e.g., how to obtain photoduplication services, the location of centers at other nearby institutions with very much larger or specialized facilities).

Because manuals tend to become outdated rather rapidly, some colleges provide them in a loose-leaf format and sell them, with periodic supplements, through the campus bookstore.

STAFF REQUIREMENTS

What staff will the center's director need? The nature of this staff depends on the services to be provided. How it will be organized and what names and titles are given to the various parts of it are matters the director may decide for himself. Most such staffs look alike and can be described in fairly general terms.

There is a feeling on some campuses that the director is constantly expanding his staff in order to build an empire of overpaid people. This is not necessarily true. The director is acutely aware—probably more than anyone else on campus—of what his center costs the college and what it takes to get full value from that amount of money. He must have a staff adequate to satisfy what he understands to be the college's requirements. As the range of users increases, and as the center gets busier, the staff will naturally grow—though not necessarily proportionately. Many directors eventually develop three basic groups—one for operations, one for administrative data processing, and another for scientific programming.

Operations

For a medium-to-large installation, a manager of operations will be needed. (When the center is small, the director himself may perform this function.) The manager will supervise the computer operators, keep track of the ordering of supplies, and see that proper accounts are kept of equipment and computer time charges. He will deal with the maintenance personnel and be responsible for scheduling. He will have had experience as an operator and a programmer. His responsibilities, however, are primarily managerial and not technical. He keeps the shop going on a business-like day-to-day basis.

The computer operators are responsible to the director of operations. The number will depend on the size of the computer, the number of operating hours per day, and on whether the center operates as an open or closed shop. These operators generally have a high school diploma, a few months of training, and considerable natural ability and energy. The use of part-time help is widespread. Student help may be seriously considered if turnover does not make the cost of retraining excessive and the work load correlates with the seasonal availability of students on campus.

Analysis and Programming

In performing the tasks necessary to move from a statement of a problem to a machine operating on the solution of that problem, a distinction is frequently made between two stages of operation: analysis and programming. The actual point at which analysis ends and programming begins is not always sharply defined. Conceptually, however, the distinction is clear. The analyst converts the user's statement of the problem to a clear and unambiguous form and further makes a statement (in some computer-oriented form) of how the program will operate to solve the problem. How detailed this statement is varies with custom and the individuals involved. The programmer reduces the analyst's statements to machine instruction, tests them against sample data, and corrects his program until it will perform the functions stated in the analyst's specification and will accommodate the total range of expected inputs. He also must provide complete *documentation* for other users or for those who may wish to modify the program for other purposes.

If the center is to provide any really useful assistance to faculty users, a group will probably exist to serve the foregoing functions. It may consist of only one senior programmer who helps out when users have programming problems beyond their ability. He will advise them but not do the work for them. At the other end of the spectrum, a college with many users who do not wish to do their own programming and who can afford professional help (in funded research, for example) will have a staff of analysts and programmers to do the actual work of the ultimate user, converting his specifications of requirements into computer code, checking the program out, and even running the job.

If the analysts and programmers for administrative applications are to be part of the center, they will form another group. How large the staff is will normally depend on how much work is planned for simultaneous implementation. Normally, a man will work on only one job at a time, with some overlap with others at the beginning and end of the process.

It may be thought peculiar that there should be two analysis and programming staffs, one for scientific and the other for administrative applications. The two kinds of applications are different in some ways and frequently attract people with different talents. Analysis of business data processing problems sometimes demands comprehension of rather fuzzy statements of requirements, getting consensus among a number of users, and understanding how complex interpersonal systems (such as registration) actually work to design a feasible and economic system to perform each specified function. The scientific analyst is more often presented with clearer problems, generally by a single user, for programs of some internal complexity (frequently involving sophisticated mathematics). His problem is to design a best solution, but purely economic considerations are generally not as pertinent as in the case of business problems. However, migration between the two staffs is by no means rare, and such migrations have considerable value since the two fields can often profit from cross-fertilization.

Organizational Structure

The organizational aspects of a typical center—obviously a moderately large one—are shown in Figure 2. In many places, the boxes may be null sets or represent only a part-time service.

Note the bicameral committee structure. The policy committee represents major administrative and academic interests. The user's group is primarily technical and may include even student users. The administrative assistant may be a secretary or a technical aide to the director, handling routine administrative details of the center's operation and leaving the director free to perform his primarily intellectual and leadership functions. There may be more than one operator, depending on the size of the computer and the number of hours of operation, but there is usually a senior operator on every shift. Auxiliary services include keypunching, accessory machine operation, checking results, and providing courier service. Members of the analysis staff, especially in larger colleges, may be drawn from the various administrative departments and provided with training in analysis; in some colleges, these departments employ their own system analysts who thus do not work for the center's director. Consultants provide the services discussed earlier in this report and may also function as instructors or tutors if there is no departmentalized instruction in programming.

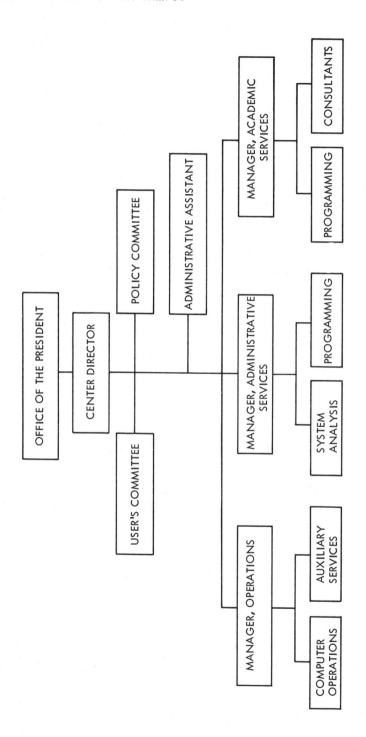

FIGURE 2: ORGANIZATION OF A TYPICAL CENTER

Staff Identification

It may at first appear preferable to base the staff for administrative applications in the using departments rather than in the computer center and to let the registrar, admissions officer, and comptroller, for example, each have his own system analyst or programmer. This is usually impractical except in very large institutions, because the needs of each officer are too small to warrant exclusive use of even one programmer. But the apparent desirability of such a practice warrants further discussion.

The data processing personnel can solve the problems of the administrative offices only in a very limited sense. They can supply the technological expertise, but the expertise in the substantive field (admissions, registration, faculty records, budgeting) can be supplied only by the cognizant officers of the college. A system to satisfy needs in any of these areas can only be built by a very close cooperation between these officers and the analysts. It is essential that the analyst *identify* with the office for which he is working. He can usually do this best by actually working in that office. Indeed, in many cases it has proved more beneficial to teach junior members of these departments the new technical skills than to import professional analysts and programmers and teach them the needs of the administrative offices.

What Wasserman says about libraries is true of most administrative offices:

Data processing is one rapidly advancing modern technological response to the growing and burdensome work routines of academic libraries. While those skilled in harnessing it to library requirements are essential to orderly advance, it should be well understood . . . that technical experts perform in staff roles as subordinates to administrative generalists. It is the technical expert who counsels, advises, and expedites.[1]

The responsibility of the data processing person is to be sure that the decisions made are technically sound; he cannot be held responsible for decisions about the true objectives and functions of the admissions officer, the registrar, the librarian, or anyone else.

Acquiring the Staff

At many institutions acquiring and retaining a competent staff poses acute problems. Many administrators are reluctant to spend

[1] Paul Wasserman, *The Librarian and the Machine* (Detroit: Gale Research Co., 1965), p. 88.

money on good people, but their presence may increase the effectiveness of the work done by the computer by as much as fifty percent. Some installations might well get more work done by trading in their computer for a smaller one and using the savings to hire more competent people to run it. But some donors and legislators (and some college presidents) are more impressed by a gleaming set of hardware with an expensive and prestigious price tag than by the quiet, sometimes expensive, and often disturbingly young people who understand today's computers. Yet there is nothing more ludicrous than having a computer costing several thousand dollars a month run badly or used foolishly because the college would not spend a thousand dollars a month for another good programmer or analyst to exploit the equipment fully. The reluctance of colleges to hire these experts at the salaries they ask is understandable, but they are at a premium, and some incentive is necessary to get them (and keep them) away from industry. The prestige of working for a college is not usually enough to attract nor hold them. In this dynamic and fast growing field, much of the exciting research and worthwhile new developments are occurring in industrial laboratories. Thus industry can offer intellectual stimulation equal to that of the college and can sometimes offer improved salaries and benefits.

Some colleges, unwilling to hire experienced programmers, train some of their junior administrators in programming. This does not always solve the problem. The consequence, not infrequently, is that the junior administrator, after a few months of experience in programming, is offered a substantial increase to go to work elsewhere. The college has converted him into the marketable commodity they were unwilling to buy and now must pay the going rate anyway or lose him.

Students who know programming are frequently hired on a part-time basis as programmers for either scientific or administrative applications. This has several temporary advantages: student labor is handy and inexpensive; sometimes student programmers are very talented and will do extraordinary work. On the other hand, students eventually go away, sometimes even before a job is finished, and often before it is sufficiently documented so that someone can complete it. Furthermore, their work is always second in priority to their studies and will suffer at crucial points in the year (as at examination time). It is the feeling of many colleges who have tried to use student programmers that such help is very useful for trying out new ideas, especially when the implementation of these ideas has a low priority. One college had a student write a prediction program for its development office. This would have been too fanciful and uncertain an undertaking to pay a more costly professional or consultant to do; the student wrote it at very low cost. If the project had been unsuccessful (it was not), little would have been lost. A further conclusion is that if students are to be relied upon heavily, in order to get a lot of work done at little cost, some of the money saved should be invested in a competent person to manage them. He can assure some continuity and some guarantees of quality and documentation.

The college should not overlook the potential supply of useful assistance in the wives of graduate students and younger faculty members. It is possible to recruit intelligent young women, with or without a college degree, who can be trained in a relatively short time and who can do some of their work at home. Much programming work is perfectly suitable for part-time work and at an off-site location. Some of the best programmers to be found in computer centers today are young women.

As involved as some of this may sound, the essential point has to be faced: even the best computer will do only what its human users tell it to do, and *there is no substitute for high quality—and close association with the system—in the human elements of a computing establishment.*

PAYING FOR THE WORK

The problem of how to support computer centers is often a very complex one which varies with the individual situation of the college. Here only some of the major issues will be discussed.[2] The acquisition of a computer is not a one-time expense. Even if it is purchased, maintenance, supplies, operations, and programming are on-going expenses; furthermore, in a few years the computer may have to be replaced by new equipment. A major question, therefore, is how these on-going

[2] *Digital Computer Needs in Colleges and Universities* (Washington: Committee on Uses of Computers, National Academy of Sciences, 1966), commonly referred to as the Rosser report, provides a thorough and lucid account of the question of computer financing in colleges from which some of the information presented here derives. See especially Chapter 5, "Funding Procedures and Costs."

expenses are to be budgeted. A technique is needed which will be fair to all the users, which will encourage worthwhile use while screening out those applications that could be performed as easily with less expensive equipment. Several methods are now employed; none seems to satisfy all these criteria.

Indirect Costing

The small college acquiring its first computer and planning to use it for numerous jobs throughout the institution often pays for it through some general fund. To attempt to charge specific departments and administrative offices for their fair share of the costs seems foolish. It will be treated much like the library—as a general resource available to any user in the college. No one would suggest direct charging of library services to every user nor attempt to regulate use of the library according to ability to pay. The argument for indirect charging for computer service is considered sound not only in small colleges but in several major universities as well. There are several arguments for this method of financing:

1. It is simple. It avoids the detailed, complex, and expensive bookkeeping involved in allocating use to various cost centers. If the college is to pay all or a large share of the costs in the long run, it is certainly easier to have one lump sum in the budget than to have a small item for computing in the budget of several dozen departments and offices.

2. It avoids some of the thorny problems of the alternatives discussed below. The major one is that a few colleges find it difficult to reach agreement on the fair cost of computer time or to predict usage accurately. Operation and maintenance are known costs, but some colleges have little precedent for charging for space occupancy, electricity, and amortization of equipment.

3. It encourages people to use the machine. Faculty, students, and administrators will feel free to experiment with applications in new areas if they are allowed easy access to the computer; if they receive a bill every time they approach the machine, they may well be more diffident.

There are, however, some corresponding disadvantages to indirect costing: First, although the college will want to encourage use when its computer center is new and little used, this situation will change.

When the center becomes overloaded, they will want to encourage worthwhile applications and discourage trivia. Some administrative applications may not seem economically justifiable, if strict cost justification is required. Some may actually be cheaper to do by hand, at least for a while. Some research use is subject to the same criticism. One way to ensure that thought is given to the question is to ask individual users to budget their computer time. If a scientist must choose between a laboratory assistant and so many hours of computer time, he will be encouraged to weigh their relative value.

A second difficulty is that indirect charges are actually being made to all departments, whether or not they are using the computer. This will be particularly noticeable at institutions at which there is funded research. The cost of computing will be part of the overhead of every research contract, whether or not computer use is involved. Some government agencies, moreover, prefer to see direct charges for computer time and will not accept indirect charging. Several large institutions have been able to continue indirect charging in spite of the obstacles, but it seems uncertain whether the government agencies who support them with contracts will allow this to continue.

Direct Costing

Some colleges have found it preferable to run their computer center as a self-supporting service bureau. Departments who plan to use the center must budget for it. The center supplies itself with the equipment and manpower it expects to be able to sell, and it is run like a small business.

It is argued by some administrators that constructing a budget forces the user to think carefully about what he wants and what part of his resources he can commit to meet what needs. As one vice-president put it:

When someone thinks he needs to use the computer, I want him to estimate fairly carefully what it's worth to him. I also want him to prepare carefully for the time he uses and write good programs so that he won't waste our money fumbling with poorly conceived experiments with computer time. I don't believe in charging students for necessary work, but I want each department to recognize that if computing is an essential part of the instructional program it's an essential item in the budget and that they should support student use accordingly.

Direct costing further places the responsibility of justifying the expense of computer services on the user rather than on the computer center staff. With a direct charging system, users must estimate their needs and stay within their estimates. If their estimates appear high, it is they who must justify their requirements and not the computer center director. "I'm not going to fight for that money," one director said. "If the user really needs it, let him fight for it."

Nor does this charging method necessarily discourage new users. If the computer center director wants to keep in the black and keep growing, he will go out and solicit business. If computer time is offered free to all comers, he is eventually forced to discourage some new users.

If the computer is a large one, or if there are several, questions multiply. Should the user be charged for the entire cost of the center or only those pieces of equipment he uses? If special equipment is acquired for various projects and becomes part of the center, it is clearly unfair for every user to pay for this. Special rates will be required. Special services may be needed, and this will also affect rates. Some research projects may require immediate computer time, on demand, to process data as they are produced, while other users are able to wait. Such service is clearly more valuable and should cost more. But how *much* more should it cost? In short, attempts to be fair may make the costing procedures impractically complex, and practical inequities may develop.

Mixed Methods

Between these two extremes, numerous alternatives have been tried. One institution Solomonically divides the question neatly in half. Such indirect costs as amortization, space, and utilities are part of the institutional overhead and are not charged to the user. Direct costs such as salary, equipment rental and maintenance, and supplies are charged directly to users. The same rates apply to everyone, and everyone is billed. Approved student use is charged to the student's department, which has to pay for it.

One state university has established a rate based on cost to the university of the computer and services but sells its services to different customers at different rates: one for research done for commercial organizations, a second to other state agencies, a third to government-sponsored research projects, a fourth to other colleges in the area, and a fifth to students and unsponsored faculty research. Different types of customers, not different types of service, are charged on the basis of presumed obligation or ability to pay. There has always been some question as to whether this was fair; it has been declared unacceptable to government agencies in U.S. Bureau of the Budget Circular A-21, which specifies policies for charging for equipment used in work supported by federal research grants and contracts. It does not mention computers specifically; hence there has been some discussion and varying interpretation. Basically, however, the government's intent is clear. Varying rates are acceptable for varying services, but for the same service the government will pay no more than any other user. Before the enunciation of this policy, several institutions which did a great deal of government-sponsored research found it possible to charge all the costs of the computer center to government contracts; the educational uses and unsponsored research were then free. This may no longer be possible.

Some concessions have been made on these points as a result of an arbitrated dispute between the federal government and the Carnegie Institute of Technology, sometimes referred to as the *Carnegie decision*. Essentially, the present effect of this ruling is to approve the charging of different rates for different classes or qualities of service rather than for different classes of users. For example, a user who is willing to wait a day for his results can justifiably be charged less than one who wants service within the hour, and the user who is willing to come in at 3 a.m. Sunday may with some justice (and sympathy) be charged less than one who wants service during prime time (in the middle of the week). Other possible exceptions include use of only a portion of the equipment (the central processor) with no requirement for auxiliary storage or remotely located data-gathering devices.[3]

One of the basic points of dispute is the status of educational discounts offered by some machine vendors. The intent of such discounts is to permit colleges to afford equipment which students could learn to use. This is not done entirely out of charity of course; the vendor's intent is to encourage students to become familiar with (if not affectionate toward) their line of equipment, in the hope that in

---

[3] A more technical explanation of these points is contained in the Defense Contract Audit Agency's Regulation 7640.9, a copy of which may be obtained from the Department of Defense or from the National Association of College and University Business Officers (1785 Massachusetts Avenue, N.W., Washington, D.C. 20036).

later years the student will want his employer to acquire such equipment. The federal government has argued that such discounts are not charitable contributions and that the college must use the actual rental cost, not the prediscount cost, in determining hourly rates. The manufacturer argues that the government's policy defeats the manufacturer's purpose of enabling colleges to offer free services to students.

Whatever the outcome of the current (1967) struggle to obtain further government concessions on this matter, it is worth taking a short look at the basic fact that Rate=Cost/Time. The more time effectively used, the lower the rate, if cost remains constant. If free time cannot be given to students, because then the government cannot be charged a higher rate, students or departments without funds cannot use the computer, and the number of hours of useful time decreases. One does not have to be an economist to see that rates must then rise—which further aggravates the problem. One large university was so adversely affected by this policy that it exhausted its year's budget for student computer time in the first three months of the fiscal year.

THE HEALTHY CENTER

One of the central messages of this report is that the top administrators of the college must know enough about computers to understand their functions and potentials in higher education and to be able to make decisions about the nature and service of computer centers. Such knowledge need not be very detailed nor technical. Since the president is not usually a technician but must rely on technicians, he may sometimes worry about the state of health of the computer center at his college. Is it being run properly and efficiently? Could improvements be made? Are we headed for a major crisis, or are things really running smoothly? Can the president recognize danger signals without being a computer technician?

Good Centers and Bad

Healthy computer centers have some common characteristics which the president (or the interested outside observer) can recognize:

1. The healthy center has a wide base of users, including many departments using a variety of services.

2. Many students take an active interest in the computer, and some of them establish, on their own, an informal or formal group to learn about computers and discuss them. Some will haunt the center as much as they are tolerated, sometimes volunteering services —and certainly advice.

3. Users are enthusiastic and encourage their colleagues to use the computer. Such users may teach noncredit courses in programming with their colleagues in mind—"Computer Programming in Chemistry," "Programming in Sociology," "Programming Engineering Applications," and so on.

4. The computer center receives support from the administration, but not blind support. There is discussion at all levels about the function of the computer in the college. One frustrated computer center director said, "It isn't enough to double my budget every year; we want them to understand what we're doing."

5. Less than half of the computer time used is devoted to running programs already written and checked out (production runs). The testing of new problems and revised systems occupies a prominent share of the work load.

6. The president will, through informal contacts with students, staff, and faculty, hear complaints, but most users will understand the problems of the center and know why their demands cannot always be satisfied.

7. The healthy center publishes periodic reports documenting such things as who the users are, what they are doing, how much time the computer is used, its budget, and what is being accomplished.

The most highly regarded centers seem to have emerged in situations in which both administrators and faculty feel strongly that the computer and its functions are a vital part of the whole educational program, in terms of both content and methodology. Such integration seems to be most evident when the president and the top leadership of the institution take the lead in establishing objectives and standards—and especially attitudes. Such leadership responsibility may certainly be delegated to some extent, but it cannot successfully be avoided if the computer is to take its proper place in the life of the college.

Models of Failure

There are some danger signs which will indicate to the president that the center may be headed for trouble, even though the center officially reports no trouble:

First there is the *one man syndrome*. The observer is told that Mr. X (probably the director of the center, possibly his right-hand man) keeps everything in his head. No one knows the answers to questions but Mr. X. If Mr. X were to become ill or take a vacation, everything would collapse.

Closely related is the problem of misplaced power. The computer center director has absolute authority to allocate the resources of the center. This gives him power of life and death over all those using the center. Because he can tell the administrative officers of the college what is and is not possible for them to do with their data, he has a stranglehold on administrative information. Although his name is fairly low on the organization chart, he is more powerful than a dean or vice-president. He controls what information the president and trustees are given.

A breakdown in communication between the technical people and administration is a sign of future troubles. Even when resources are abundant and capacities exceed needs, the flow of information to top administration tapers off, and avenues of control seem congested. When demand increases and problems arise, no mechanism will exist for the administration to understand or control the situation.

No computer operation is without problems, both current and foreseeable. If the administrator is not aware of these problems and how they are being handled, a breakdown in communication already exists. If users and potential users (particularly in administrative offices) are baffled or frustrated by their attempts to use the computer center, it is not offering the services it should.

Presidents, as part of their normal work, must listen to groans and complaints about a variety of matters, and the administrator may become hardened to what he comes to regard as barrack-room griping. However, if dark remarks about the computer center are heard consistently, it may be well to ask an outside visitor or paid consultant to take a look at the operation and quiz some typical users. It is a very bad sign, for example, to hear that members of the faculty consistently and with no apparent reason go off campus for computer services. Computer services are too costly not to be reviewed periodically. Those responsible for the trouble may be reluctant to bring it to the president's ear; they may even be unaware of it themselves.

The Growth of the Center

One sure sign of a healthy computer center is that it periodically becomes regarded as too small. If the computer has been on the campus for more than a year or two and there is idle time during the day, either the college acquired a much larger computer than it needed or something is deterring healthy growth.

The consistent experience of many colleges is that even the most apparently exaggerated predictions of growth turn out later to have been underestimates. Growth is not desirable for its own sake, but the computer center must grow enough to keep up with and anticipate legitimate demands for service. The long lead time in obtaining hardware and personnel makes it imperative not to wait for crises to develop. It is certainly a sign of poor planning if the president hears that a center is already operating 24 hours a day and yet no one is making plans to increase the college's computing resources!

Growth may not be constant and steady, of course. A graph showing the record of utilization (usually expressed in hours per day or week) may show a very jagged line. Growth seems to go up for a year or more and then taper off or sag. Some of this irregularity may stem from seasonal variation, but in the long run it more often occurs when the center is so overloaded that growth is no longer possible, or when new and faster equipment allows the same amount of work to be done in less time.

Estimates of what constitutes a healthy average rate of growth vary. Different kinds of institutions will react differently. One thing is clear: the growth rate does not usually decrease proportionately as the center gets larger and as users become more experienced. A good rule-of-thumb is the frequently quoted figure of 40 percent growth from each previous year in computing use—which means almost doubling in two years. The comptroller at one of the largest private universities observed that this has held at his institution for a number of years—until last year, when the figure jumped to 100 percent! "And the end is not in sight," he added.

In evaluating progress, it should be stressed that growth is not a *necessary* virtue under all conditions. Again a library analogy may be helpful. The library may be said to grow healthily as long as it keeps up with the needs of its users for current resources, assuming users make reasonable demands and know their fields well enough to know what to expect. It is possible to imagine a class of users who are perfectly satisfied with the service because they don't know that anything better is available—or because they lack initiative.

Perhaps the best approach to reviewing growth is to ask: are our computer resources keeping up with legitimate and informed demands for service about as well as do those of institutions of comparable size, quality, aspirations, and affluence? The answer will always be to some extent subjective and equivocal. At worst, knowing that the question will be asked, and that evidence may be requested to support an answer, it may keep those responsible for computer leadership on their toes. The latter are responsible for meeting the needs imposed by environmental growth. But in the final analysis it is the user community (staff, faculty, and students) which bears the final responsibility for knowing enough to demand resources adequate to the needs of the institution, assuming that it wishes not only to keep up with the Joneses but to set an example of academic leadership.

THE FUTURE ENVIRONMENT

As THE COMPUTER has come to be used more widely, it has gradually lost its early identification with mere mathematics and with arithmetic calculation for scientific purposes. It is now used for processing all kinds of information. As this capability is more fully exploited, it is seen more and more as a natural ally of education and an essential tool in educational institutions. Just as it has played a vital role in military command and control, industrial management, process control, and science, the computer is now an integral tool of higher education. The trend has been for a computer use to be adopted on a hundred or more additional campuses each year and for the usage of any single campus to double every two or three years. Many factors account for this staggering growth. While the college faculty, staff, and students are investigating new ways of using computers, research laboratories produce new kinds of systems which make still further applications possible and which promise to make experimental applications economically feasible on a large scale.

In this chapter, we shall attempt to look ahead five to ten years and speculate about what the computer might look like and be doing on the campus of tomorrow. With computers, it is possible to predict some very general directions of future progress; specific achievements and rates of accomplishment are more intractable. General tendencies are always easier to predict than are specific facts. Research studies are investigating a number of areas; it is clear that some of them (but not which of them) will succeed. In predicting time scales, the imagination is usually too weak; even the wildest predictions in the computer field have usually been outrun by actuality.

In this report, we are not interested in looking into the future to see either the end of the process or the predicted situation on a specific date; we wish to focus on the situation which might exist in the 1970-1975 time period, partly to clarify what is going on today, but mostly to help the administrator plan the future of the computer on his campus. To begin, we will try to imagine the way in which hardware and software may be expected to develop.

HARDWARE VS. SOFTWARE

The most significant trends in the development of computer hardware over the past years have been lower cost per unit of work done; greater speed of computation and of access to data in storage; greater inner capacity, but with reduced physical size; and greater reliability and reduced maintenance cost. And, of course, the number of computers in operation increases—and at an increasing rate.

Some changes along these dimensions have been very dramatic. Exact figures are hard to quote, since the several *hundred* available computers vary widely and since the changes are liable to be sudden and uneven rather than gradual. One can quote some rough figures, however. On the average, cost per unit of computation seems to decrease at the rate of twenty percent per year. Speeds of machines new to the market increase tenfold every five years. The capacity (and the meaning of "small," "medium," and "large") also increases roughly tenfold about every five years. Today's "small" computer, for example, has more memory capacity and greater speed, occupies less space, and costs less than the "large" machine of the 1950's.

The case of computer memories has been one of the most dramatic. In the early 1950's, the fastest available memories had access times of several hundred microseconds; by 1955, the figure was down to about ten; by 1960 it was four. Today core memories are available with a half-microsecond (500-nanosecond) access time. The end of this development is not yet reached. It is realistic to predict memories operating at the ten-nanosecond rate in the foreseeable future. (In ten nanoseconds, an electronic impulse can travel almost ten feet!) At the same time that speed has so greatly increased, cost has gone down from the ten to fifteen dollars per character of storage of 1950 to about one dollar today. And the ten-nanosecond memory of the future may cost less than ten cents per character!

The decrease in physical size has also been exponential. The basic unit of electronic circuitry in the tube machine of ten years ago was about the size (but perhaps of greater complexity) of a table radio of the same period. With the introduction of transistors, the size was reduced to that of a pack of cigarettes. Contemporary methods have reduced this still further—to the size of a match head.

Physical size may seem a trivial aspect of the computer, but it actually is closely related to both cost and speed. Tube machines and most transistor machines were made by hand, each circuit being individually wired. New components so small as to elude the naked eye must obviously be mass produced and mechanically assembled. Their price is lower, and their standards of reliability are higher. The relationship between size and speed is made clear if one realizes that a nanosecond—the common unit of measure of the speed of tomorrow's computers—is about the time it takes electricity to pass through a foot of wire. (The size of the machine affects speed in the same direct way that the size of a campus affects time between classes.)

These developments have several important consequences for the user. They make small computers (on today's scale) very economical. Even today's moderately large computers may be so cheap in five to ten years that it will be possible for certain types of users to have their own rather than to have to work in a time-sharing mode. One can envision the day when a small office computer will be as common as today's adding machine and when fairly large computers will be used in laboratories as process-control devices. Although time-sharing of very large systems still promises to serve the majority of users for small simple jobs, long time-consuming operations (such as laboratory control) may well be done on individual computers. Another consequence of the increase in capacity, speed, and reliability, and of the decrease in cost per unit of computation, is that still larger machines become feasible for jobs which are simply too big for today's machines (there are many such jobs) or for extremely large time-sharing systems.

INPUT/OUTPUT EQUIPMENT

A major problem in the use of computers has always been the interface between man and the machine. To this problem an intensive research and development effort is currently being applied. The two necessary developments which will probably most affect the use to which the computer will be put are a reasonably priced and sophisticated visual reader for characters and a reasonably priced visual display device.

Currently, most input is effected by punched cards. Documents are read by a human operator and typed into a machine which punches a card. Depending on the level of reliability desired, this process can cost on the order of one-fourth to one-half cent per character. Since the cost is almost totally for labor, it cannot be expected to decrease. There are other disadvantages to the punched card such as limited size (only 80 or 90 characters per card), limited fonts and character set (fewer than 50 symbols), and awkwardness and slowness of conversion. The fastest equipment for reading cards operates at about 2,000 cards per minute; this can probably be improved very little. The most promising device to break the keypunch bottleneck is the print reader. Devices are now available which will read 2,000 characters per second, but under considerable restriction: the documents must be very clear, of good contrast, and of a limited and prespecified font of type. Some of these machines can, however, convert printed matter at a cost on the order of fractions of a cent per character; however, they cannot be used to convert existing files, such as library cards and student records to machine-readable form, which are generally too variable in format to be accepted. It seems possible, however, that the versatility of such machines will rise (and their price go down) in the next decade.

The output capabilities of early computers—and, indeed, of most computers today—were limited to a printer with a character set of 47 (the same as the keypunch) and a line of about 120 characters, but numerous improvements have been made. Some computers today have *plotters* which read or print graphs or diagrams. Some work is being done in linking some form of document-reproducer to the computer so that it will be possible to retrieve copies of prestored documents. Perhaps the most versatile output device is the CRT (cathode ray tube), on the face of which the computer can write (display) visual information to be read immediately by the user. This form of storage is not permanent. The user can regenerate the display at any time, but there is nothing to take away. It does, however, offer great capabilities for the on-line user who wants to work with the machine to achieve some objective which can later be recorded by other means. Such users usually use a typewriter keyboard to communicate with the machine, and associated CRT displays are available (but expensive).

At the far-out edge of the research laboratory, there are now prototypes of devices which will permit manuscript and vocal inputs and outputs. The RAND tablet, a 10-inch square of very thin cross-hatched wires, permits one to write or draw images which the computer immediately reads and translates into usable form. These images can then be immediately repeated on the CRT display for editing. A three-dimensional figure may be drawn in this way, and then the computer can alter its perspective or rotate it for viewing at different angles. One program exists which can be used to teach the computer the user's handwriting, using upper and lower case letters, numbers, special symbols, and non-English alphabets. After a few tries, the computer recognizes each of the varying ways the user writes the letter H or the number 4; it stores this information and uses it to interpret writing on the RAND tablet. At one telephone research laboratory, a device already exists which can recognize most of the phonemes of spoken English, and if it recognizes them it will not be long before signals can be produced which are usable by a computer. These patterns can be recreated electronically, and it is perfectly feasible to imagine carrying on a *vocal* conversation with tomorrow's computer.

Needless to say, the college should not expect all of these developments to appear on the market shortly. But it should be noted that for many years there will continue to be new developments which will enlarge the scope of computer applications and which will affect the college's own plans for the computer. These developments, simplifying the problems of getting information into and out of the computer, together with the larger and cheaper memories of the future, will allow users to store vastly larger quantities of information in the computer and to interrogate at will. It will be possible, for instance, to store long passages in natural language data which can be indexed manually (or automatically) and browsed through by the computer. This range of application is sure to be one of the most important (particularly for academic institutions) in future years.

SOFTWARE

In attempting to describe the changes which can be expected from computers, and the impact that these changes may have on the user, it is perhaps an artificial distinction to speak separately of hardware and software. The developments that will take place in greater convenience and power for the user (which today one normally associates with the software aspect of the system) may well be implemented by hardware techniques rather than intermediate programming. But it is not of importance to the user how the change is accomplished, just as it is not important what specific device will appear to make computers cheaper. He cares only how the system will look to him, what aspect it will present to him when he approaches it. Three developments in this area seem particularly significant: *time-sharing systems, new languages,* and *general-purpose information handling systems.*

Time-sharing systems were discussed briefly in an earlier chapter. Such systems are only beginning to emerge from the research laboratory. Their impact on the vast majority of users has not begun to be felt. A computer used in this way is so different from a computer used in the batch-processing mode that the user's habits are profoundly affected. Even the uses of the computer gradually change. Its salient features are its convenience (a terminal in the user's office or down the hall rather than in another building), responsiveness and immediacy (one deals with the computer himself rather than through an operator), and speed of reaction (on the order of seconds rather than hours or days). For many users, the time-shared system becomes an integral tool of thought rather than an accessory resource. It becomes (to return to the familiar analogy) more like his personal office library and less like a public library with closed stacks.

The earliest developments of higher-order languages (such as

FORTRAN and COBOL) permitted the user to direct the computer in a form of language more familiar to him than the special language of the computer; the model was the formula used by the scientist or the accountant. Current developments offer marked improvements in these general languages as well as in new, special-purpose languages. For many potential users, the sophisticated capabilities of general-purpose languages only make the language (and thus the computer) more difficult to master. Languages are being developed which bring the computer closer to the user with a special range of subject matter in mind (statistical analysis, the writing of programmed instruction, or the construction or modification of document in natural language, for example). Such languages are often developed in the context of time-sharing systems in that they assume that the user is typing his inputs as he is thinking about the problem and not after he has already thought out what he has to say. The systems interact with the user, immediately pointing out procedural errors in his input and even explaining aspects of the system with which he may be unfamiliar.

A very common use of the computer is to maintain a large file of structured information, sometimes called a data base. Most systems doing this kind of work were constructed for a single application and are not very flexible. It has gradually become apparent, however, that such systems have much in common and that considerable cost and effort could be saved by building general-purpose data management systems. Such systems have been constructed experimentally and are now coming into wider use. They allow the user to specify the format of his information, make changes in and additions to it, and request specific outputs from it. Such systems also permit easy manipulation of the data, providing not only for retrieval of information already in the file, but also for projections of new data from what already exists. Such systems have been used, for example, in systems for personnel data, inventory control, document retrieval, and files of engineering data supporting large developmental projects. The uses for file management systems on campus are innumerable: faculty records, property inventories, student records, library acquisitions, support of research (to replace, perhaps, the ubiquitous 5x8 filing card), maintenance of the college's historical information as a basis for planning.

THE COLLEGE ENVIRONMENT

As these developments take place, computers will affect many aspects of our society. One of the significant consequences of the growing use of computers is to change the environment of the college, the world of which it is a part. One of the pressures colleges will feel (and indeed many have already felt it) is from the entering freshman. Computers are a very lively topic in high school. In fact, computer programming has been taught experimentally as early as the fifth grade. In the next decade, the entering freshman, particularly if his interests are science-oriented, will more frequently arrive with some knowledge of computer programming. He will consider the computer an ordinary and indispensable device which he needs and expects, just as today's freshman takes for granted those other gadgets (typewriters, television, tape recorders, interlingual dictionaries, slide rules, and library card catalogs) which were novelties at one time. He will consider the college ill-equipped which does not supply such basic tools of education.

As more colleges begin to use computers as a tool of institutional research and amass more data on their history and operations, federal agencies become more interested in gathering these data together to study educational trends in the country as a whole. As more questionnaires probe more deeply into the details of the college's functioning, the need to maintain detailed records and to be able to retrieve reports from this fund of information is increasing. It is hard to see any decrease in this trend.

As information becomes unwieldy in volume and complexity, computers can be employed to simplify data handling. But when the task becomes easier, more information can be maintained and required. A never-ending spiral is created, which some people have compared to the relationship of superhighway construction and automobile population. One stimulates the other.

We have mentioned the entering freshman. The departing senior is also part of the college's environment. The college graduate enters a world in which computers play a large part. Most well-educated men will be expected to know something of their characteristics and use. They need not be trained technicians obviously, but they will need to know what can be done with computers. This is true in the fields of academic scholarship, business, government, and the military, as well as of engineering and the sciences. The college graduate of the mid-1970's will live in a world in which men are everywhere aided by information-handling machines which he will need to understand. He will, after all, be a leader in his field in the twenty-first century.

theless the w'   .d routine use of b   r in the
American   still several year'

Befor   ens, the cost
of equi'   t become man-
agea'   ut foundation
sub'   a more important,
so'   universities must
y'   are centralized com-
             ilities.
        this happens, students
    able to "dial" lessons,
   essions, and entire plays
  oncerts for "use" in class-
ms, study halls or even dor-
itory rooms and homes. A
small-scale experiment of such
central computer "libraries" is
now under way in West Hartford and Hartford, Conn.
The present problem, apart
from cost, is the lack of programs—materials to be fed into
the computers. It is relatively
easy to commission a textbook,
but there is as yet no adequate
supply of able academicians who
are also at home with computer
programing.

Computer: Instrument of Change

Computers:
Instruments
For Change

Computers:
New Values
For Mankind

COMPUTERS ON TOMORROW'S CAMPUS

In many ways, the effect on campus of the changes described in the preceding chapter is obvious; the reader can be left to imagine on his own a scenario of a day in the life of the college in the late twentieth century. Three specific areas, however, seem worthy of more detailed investigation: computer-aided instruction;[1] information retrieval; and total administrative systems. These are the areas in which the most intensive research and development are now taking place. Manufacturers of computers and peripheral devices, academic and industrial laboratories, and government agencies are seeking and finding solutions to the technical problems. Actual operational systems in these three areas are under construction or in use on campuses across the country. The chief current barrier to implementing such systems is the cost and availability of hardware, and this problem is gradually being eased. There are also conceptual problems, as will be indicated, but these are currently under intensive study and will be solved.

INFORMATION SCIENCE AND THE LIBRARY

General-purpose information systems—in the sense in which they were discussed in Chapter 10—function in such a way as to maintain information in a structured data base and to retrieve information from it on demand. The data base itself contains descriptions, in some sense, of entities which are not a part of the system. Obviously this broad definition applies to most, if not all, systems involving the *use* of information; perhaps the best example of such a system, on campus or off, is found in a library. The card catalog is a data base which describes entities (documents, books) which exist elsewhere in the library. Indices and tables of contents in the documents themselves are bases describing the topics of the document

---

[1] The term CAI is frequently used as shorthand for computer-aided instruction.

itself. The information available in the library is thus indexed and referenced in a number of hierarchically ordered ways so as to help the user find the information in as convenient and efficient way as possible. Such a system is often vast and complex; it is used by different people in different ways and for different purposes. One book (say on electricity) is very different from another; no description will answer all the questions a potential reader might ask. A library inventory is obviously more complex than, for example, a property inventory system—one light bulb is much like another; a few parameters will describe any bulb to any potential searcher's satisfaction.

Many of the problems facing today's library are procedural and clerical in nature; some of them have been mentioned earlier. Computers are now being used in these cases. Book and periodical acquisitions are time- and money-consuming operations; they involve much paper shuffling and computers have demonstrated their usefulness as an aid. Computers are used also in charge-out systems, when the goal is to keep track of where the holdings of the library actually are. Such applications are becoming enormously important in the library; but what we wish to discuss here is a new application altogether, just appearing on the horizon: the use of computers to help people *find information.*

Today's library uses a system which has evolved over many years to help those who need information. It has existed in essentially its current form since the middle of the last century, but in those hundred years many things have affected the nature of the problem the library catalog was originally designed to solve. Some experts feel that the library system, as we know it, is no longer adequate to solve today's (much less tomorrow's) information problems. Many factors combine to aggravate the difficulties of the librarian and his clients. The rate of publications throughout the world has steadily increased as has the requirement of libraries to acquire and preserve new and old publications. The explosive growth of science has vastly increased scientific publications, especially journals and reports. Most libraries now collect a growing proportion of items which are not "books" in the usual sense and for which library procedures are in many ways ill-designed: journals, reports published by research laboratories and government agencies, audio recordings, photographs and films, maps, and manuscripts. With the growing pace of science and technology, research specialists depend more and more heavily on the ready availability of recent documents.

New Techniques

As early as 1945 it was suggested that new approaches must be taken to the solution of the information dissemination problem, utilizing modern techniques of automated information handling.[2] It seems clear now that library systems will undergo intense scrutiny and some redesign over the next quarter century. Libraries are a very precious resource, however, and there is bound to be much opposition to any radical change on the part of librarians whose valued interest in conserving things is often accompanied by conservatism of views. The innovations described below are not, by and large, likely to appear in many libraries in the coming decade, but the basic research and rethinking of requirements is already under way, and the far-sighted administrator should know what to expect. Radical innovations have been attempted and used successfully in some special-purpose libraries; many research libraries are keenly interested in these developments and plan to introduce them as rapidly as they become economically feasible.

As in any system development, the first problem is to think in terms of requirements rather than in terms of the techniques formerly used to satisfy them. In thinking about new forms of the transfer and dissemination of information, one writer in the field comments:

We should be prepared to reject the schema of the physical library—the arrangement of shelves, card indexes, check-out desks, reading rooms and so forth. That schema is essentially a response to books and to their proliferation. If it were not for books, and for the physical characteristics of books . . . , there would be no *raison d'etre* for many parts of the schema of the physical library.[3]

Another writer describes one possible mode for the transfer of information using totally new schema:

In the university of the future . . . the library will be the central facility of an information-transfer network that will extend throughout the academic community. Students and scholars will use this network to gain access to the uni-

---

[2] Vannevar Bush, "As We May Think" (*Atlantic Monthly*, August 1945), was a key paper, opening up a whole new field of study: the use of new techniques to aid man in exploiting the fund of acquired knowledge.

[3] J. C. R. Licklider, *The Library of the Future* (Cambridge: The M.I.T. Press, 1965), p. 6f.

versity's total information resources, through Touch-Tone telephones, tele-typewriter keyboards, television-like displays, and quickly made copies. The users of the system will communicate with each other as well as with the library; data just obtained in the laboratory and comments made by observers will be as easily available as the texts of books in the library or documents in the departmental files. The information traffic will be controlled by means of the university's time-shared computer utility, much as today's verbal communications are handled by the campus telephone exchange. Long-distance service will connect the university's information-transfer network with sources and users elsewhere.[4]

If the reader finds this paragraph fanciful, he should note that it appears in a prospectus for the establishment of just such a library. The fine details of such operating systems—rapid reproduction of documents by xerographic processes, microfilm and microfiche production and handling, systems of communication—are outside the scope of this study. This discussion is limited to the major implications of computer sciences for documentary sciences. The intent is not to explain in detail or to justify these proposals, but only to indicate what new possibilities the use of the computer affords to the library in the solution of problems of maintenance, use, and transfer of information.

The library envisioned in the quotations above will be achieved only in gradual stages. The first step seems to be the automation of the retrieval function—helping the user find something. If the catalog is the nerve system of the library, it is the first that will reflect the new technology. Systems have been built (one will be described below) which have done this: they accept requests for information and, with the aid of a computer, find references which may be helpful. Such systems automate, in effect, the functions served in today's library by the catalog and by the reference librarian.

A further step is the automation of the cataloging process itself. Computer-based retrieval systems require more detailed indexing than is normally available in the library's present card catalog. Techniques are being investigated for automatic indexing, based upon word frequencies, positions of key words in sentences, and so on. Closely related to this research is the investigation of automatic extraction: the creation of a brief summary of a document (similar in intent to an abstract) by extracting what seems to be the key language of a document. Such research has so far been only moderately success-

[4] Carl F. J. Overhage, "Plans for Project Index," *Science*, May 20, 1966, p. 1032.

ful, even in controlled environments. As in other areas of computer research involving the manipulation of natural languages (automatic translation, for example), it has not yet found ways of overcoming all the many kinds of vagueness and ambiguity of language with which human users have less difficulty.

Finding Information

The area which has received the greatest attention and where fruitful results have most frequently been found is information retrieval. Given an index (no matter how produced) and an unambiguous query, computer programs can match the key words of the question to the terms by which the file is described. Some such systems are very simple: the question must consist of a list of descriptors; the answer is a list of all those entries with which some of these descriptors are tagged. If one wanted, for instance, references to *the use of computers in college administration,* he would list "college," "computer," and "administration." Those documents would fall out which were tagged by those three terms (or any acceptable subset of them). Unfortunately, documents about the administration of computers at colleges or the use of computers in colleges of administration would also be acceptable to such a crudely formed request. Other systems allow more sophisticated questions, linked by logical connectors (colleges *and* universities, computers *or* information systems, computers *but not* analog computers) or for hierarchical sequences of key words.

Understanding a request for information is itself often a difficult problem. People who ask librarians for information have often only a confused or vague notion of what they want to know. They may use vague and contradictory expressions. They may use the wrong words altogether. Their questions may be so broad as to cover a subject on which the library has thousands of publications. They may be so narrow as to exclude everything. They normally do not specify the depth of interest involved: whether a specialist's work is required, an introductory text, or a handbook. The necessity for the requestor to define precisely what he wants makes the evaluation of information retrieval systems very difficult. It is not clear that anyone can yet define adequately a good computer-produced answer to any question. Consider, for example, this request: "I want reports of recent research on the effect of the x group of drugs on all primates except man."

The requestor assumes that the person or agency answering his request will understand what he means by recent, what the members of the x drug group are, and what primates includes. The paper he will be interested in seeing may not mention the word primate but only specific animals, nor need it mention drug y as being in the x group of drugs. And such a question as whether a given paper is *not* about man may involve a moderately sophisticated decision.

Further Research

Other areas of research have also been explored with fruitful results. Library systems which maintain catalogs of recent acquisitions in machine-readable form sometimes also provide selective dissemination of new information: users describe their interests with a subset of the same descriptor terms by which documents are indexed; periodically they receive a list of all new acquisitions which match their criteria. One of the most impressive implications of such systems is their ability to catalog and index journal articles as well as books—something the general scientific library has never found feasible. Thus the scope of the library information system is extended to the scientific journal, where the newest information tends to be available.

Library of Congress catalog cards are now also available on magnetic tape suitable for use in automated cataloging systems. The Library of Congress is also studying new methods of descriptive bibliography and is evaluating new equipment.

On the basis of these experiments and research, libraries are now possible which are still based on the book, journal, or document as the basic form of information transfer, but in which the catalog is, essentially, automated. Such systems now exist; some (like the MEDLARS system of the National Library of Medicine) are very successful. Numerous university libraries are considering automating at least specialized subsections of their main catalog.

It is difficult to evaluate such systems, even those which have existed long enough to be used; they are still all in either an experimental environment or special collections. None are in large, general-purpose research libraries. Experimental systems now operate on relatively small collections of documents. Systems in actual use, on the other hand, tend to be in specialized libraries where the subject matter is easier to control and where the users tend to have a great deal in common: they are all specialists in the same or related fields. They are also usually small libraries where new acquisitions are generally more important and of more interest than is the backlog collection.

A specific system now in operation will be described, since it dramatizes what is now possible. It uses a time-shared computer, with typewriter-like input-output devices and/or a cathode ray tube (CRT) display with a light-pen which allows the user to indicate his requests to the computer by pointing to items on the CRT. The system allows for considerable flexibility in organizing and structuring the classification scheme. We will mention a few of the options available to the user.

The user may approach the system in either of two modes: browsing or searching. If he decides to browse, a list of the broad categories in which the bibliographic file is organized is displayed, with a list of the *actions* he may take. If the information is presented on the CRT display, the user can select one of these options merely by pointing to it. The user examines the list of some thirty-odd categories and selects one. He points with his light-pen to the word CHEMISTRY on his display. Immediately the display is replaced by one which indicates the number of entries in the category he has selected and a list of subcategories and synonyms. He points with his pen to CHEMICAL ANALYSIS. The next display shows a similar listing of this subcategory with the number of entries and suggested subcategories and synonyms. The user may thus select the general *area* in which he is interested, while maintaining an awareness of the size of the collection. When he has reduced the area of search to the specific subjects he is interested in, he may request and see displayed abstracts of the individual documents.

If he elects the search mode rather than browsing, the user may type in the index terms he wishes, with some logical relationships. For our earlier example, he might write:

DRUG X

EFFECT

PRIMATE AND NOT MAN

The system helps him to investigate the index terms actually used. Before typing in this list, he may ask for synonyms and related terms. Documents containing his specific descriptor terms are cited. He may then choose to browse, examining the abstracts of the individual documents cited, or ask that the list be printed out for his later reference.

Such a system is experimental and operates on a catalog of only a few thousand titles. But it demonstrates the technical feasibility of allowing users to search, and in a new sense to browse, through a catalog in a novel and useful way. Only the size of available hardware and the cost of development and implementation prevent widespread use of such systems, and these limits are certain to be reduced sharply by the time today's undergraduate is an associate professor.

COMPUTER-AIDED INSTRUCTION

Computer-aided instruction utilizes the capabilities of the computer to select, present, and evaluate responses to subject matter. The student interacts with the computer through a teaching terminal which may be a typewriter-like instrument or complex display incorporating an audio system, a random-access slide projector, and a cathode ray tube. Some of the unique capacities of this instructional medium include the ability to provide:

Self-pacing—the student moves as rapidly as he can or wishes to;

Interaction with an observant and tireless "tutor";

Presentation of instructional sequences based on prior responses and other available history;

Diagnosis of weaknesses in skills and abilities that are often overlooked by human evaluators;

Basic and remedial sequences that may employ auxiliary media;

Immediate access to statistical data reflecting individual and group performance.

The computer's selective ability operates in a number of ways in adapting instruction to each student's needs. This may be accomplished by displaying material of varying difficulty, remedial reviews or exercises when responses indicate their desirability, altering sequences and presentation modes, transferring control of the machine to the learner, and giving the learner opportunities to respond in many different ways. Data obtained about the student prior to his using the terminal may affect the sequence—vocabulary, skill level, mathematical aptitude, reading comprehension levels.

Many computer-aided instruction programs have been written to provide drill and practice sequences and tutorial programs. In some respects these programs approximate the programmed instruction provided in teaching machines or programmed textbooks. However, as contrasted to the somewhat static nature of these, computer-aided instruction allows for rapid change and development. As the instructor analyzes student response, or senses adverse attitudes, sequences can be modified quickly and easily. Similarly, identification of new content to be inserted or a reassessment of academic needs can be reflected without the delay involved in the production of textbooks.

Another special dimension of the computer-aided system that has vast potential for many instructional areas is the possibility of using the information retrieval capabilities of the computer as a problem-solving tool. It has been suggested that perhaps the principal advantage of computer-aided instruction may be the greater information it can give the teacher on student performance. Because the computer can record in great detail both the student's responses and his errors, delays, and misinterpretations as well, the instructor can evaluate the performance of his instructional program as well as of his students. A scientific method now exists for the first time for the rapid evaluation and revision of educational methods and techniques. The potential of CAI in educational research has not yet begun to be more than experimentally tapped.

Prototype models of computer-based terminals in use currently offer instruction by cathode ray tubes, typewriter-like devices, motion pictures, slides, and television display screens and through headsets and microphones connected to audio tape units. The most reliable and least complicated operating terminal is the typewriter-like device. Once the typewriter was identified as having potential for instruction, components such as single cartridge film projectors and slide projectors using rear-screen projection devices and audio tape playing units were attached. As additional components have been added to more complicated terminals, their operating reliability has tended to go down, but these growing pains will eventually disappear. Originally, most of this equipment was designed for purposes other than computer-aided instruction. Currently, a device designed specifically as a computer-aided teaching terminal is in use in a major university as a part of a research study. This terminal has a CRT display, typewriter keyboard, slide, motion picture, audio, and light-pen capabilities.

The major computer manufacturers continue to explore methods for adapting to instructional purposes the general-purpose equipment presently in use for interaction with the computer. Laboratory prototype television capabilities are under investigation. Methods for rapid display of information in response to student input are also being examined. Two difficulties with the typewriter as an output device are that it prints information at less than the average reading speed and that the noise can be annoying. However, the detachable printed copy serves as a record and may be valuable to the student for review after he leaves the terminal. Consequently, as laboratory prototypes are being developed, the importance of having hard copy is being carefully evaluated.

Types of Instruction

The simplest use of CAI is in drill, in which the chief virtue of the computer is its infinite patience. Assuming that students need a great deal of practice in order to master certain basic procedures, vocabulary, skills, or facts, drill is presented in a fairly standardized fashion, and the patterns for student-computer interaction are generally limited to simple correction and retrial.

Tutorial programs are somewhat more complex. They can utilize a variety of question-and-answer sequences, presentation of reading passages, and so forth simulating student-tutor interaction. Sequences that use remedial and skip-ahead pathways determined by student responses are incorporated extensively in these programs as in programmed texts.

In simulation programs, a computer model of a physical, mathematical, or social process responds to decisions made by the student, and he receives information that shows how the simulated system was affected by his decisions. The interaction with the constantly changing configuration of the system enables the student to learn how to modify his responses to achieve a desired objective. In most such programs, prior knowledge of skills and concepts is assumed so that the student can deal with the more complex environment created by the computer. Gaming programs are also used in which the student can play actual problem-oriented games which enable him to make decisions about complicated set situations.

In problem-solving, the student must learn algorithmic or algebraic computer languages to use the computer's information file and retrieve and display data. This is less an instructional purpose than a resource that permits the student to use the computer as a problem-solving and exploratory tool or for homework and independent study.

Costs

There is currently so much variability in components that questions about the costs of computer-aided instruction are difficult to answer. There are four major ones: *terminals, line charges, computer time,* and *software.*

Terminals rent from about $100 a month (for a typewriter-like device) to about $750 a month for a CRT with keyboard and audio-visual units. These prices will certainly come down, but probably not as fast as those of computers. It is more likely that the machines will become more useful, more flexible, and more reliable, and that the prices will stay much the way they are.

Line charges are significant if the terminals are located far from the computer. Lines can be leased for about three dollars per mile per month for continuous service, or they can be made available on a toll call basis, at rates similar to those for telephone services.

Computer time, as has been indicated, will become cheaper. It is already perhaps the cheapest part of a computer-aided instructional system. Some medium-sized systems currently are able to support twelve terminals for sixty dollars an hour, or five dollars per hour per student.

A very large expense is the cost of preparing instructional software and course materials. These costs vary widely, too. Materials for one hour's student drill and practice may take a day or more to prepare. More sophisticated tutorial programs can take as long as 50 (or, according to some pessimists, as many as 200) hours of preparation per hour of instruction. The cost and difficulty of preparing a CAI course has been compared with that of preparing, testing, and producing a textbook. CAI has the advantage (and additional cost), however, that additional and more sophisticated testing is possible (in fact necessary), as it can continually be revised in use. It is like a textbook that the author never has to turn over to the printer.

An Integral Part of the Curriculum

Computer-aided instruction is of great interest to the faculty and administration in several places throughout the country. One such institution is committed to the view that the entire curriculum should function as a laboratory in which revitalization of undergraduate education and instructional experimentation are key elements of the academic program. Faculty members in many divisions and departments in this school are already engaged in the development of computer-assisted learning material. Special emphasis has been placed on controlled experimentation and evaluation as well as on course development. The instructional sequences being developed include an impressive array of difficult types of instructional material, ranging from drill routines to fairly sophisticated simulation programs. More than one hundred faculty, from all disciplines, participate in an interdivisional committee on information and communication sciences. This committee sponsors introductory computing courses and developmental testing of courses in genetics, political science, American history, and economics. Terminals are located at convenient sites across the campus, even in dormitories.

Several other colleges have approached the problem of computer-assisted instruction on a more experimental basis. Their efforts, although considerable, have not yet had a major impact on the curriculum. One college has combined its efforts to prepare curriculum materials with an evaluation of educational strategies for using CAI in technical education. During its early stages, the project utilized two terminals with electric typewriters, random-access slide projectors, and a tape recorder. These terminals are connected by telephone lines to a large computer at a research center many miles away. After preliminary experimentation, the college installed a small computer dedicated to CAI. Courses in engineering science, technical mathematics, and communication skills have been developed for two-year post-high school vocational training and for college-level courses in modern mathematics, cost accounting, audiology, and engineering economics.

One university uses computer-aided instruction to serve a variety of purposes in education and in the behavioral and physical sciences. During the past five years a computer has been used to teach a number of students simultaneously, while allowing each student to proceed independently. Exploratory studies have been undertaken in the two separate laboratories to test the capabilities of the systems while providing instruction in symbolic logic and other courses. Recently, course work in circuit analysis to cover half a semester was offered to engineering students. Other credit courses include "How to Use the Library," "FORTRAN Programming for Business and Commerce," and "Computers in Psychology." With such growing background and experience, this university is now in an excellent position to increase the number of courses offered and to increase the number of students using CAI. Thought is presently being given to a campuswide network of 2,000 teaching terminals!

Research in Teaching

More study is needed on the scope of applications of CAI, which to date has been used principally to teach facts. A thorough examination of the proper domain of CAI remains to be made. Other possible uses could include teaching interpretation, extrapolation, analysis of relationships and organizational principles, derivation of sets of abstract relations, group interaction, and judgments based upon internal evidence versus external criteria. Although computers are currently used only in teaching knowledge of specifics, there is no innate limitation which prevents their more creative use. The question of how CAI will fit into the college curriculum remains to be answered. Apparently successful experiments have produced results which need to be utilized widely in practical situations before the question can be answered.

Computer-Assisted Counseling

The computer has been used successfully (experimentally) for computer-assisted counseling. Some portions of a counselor's daily activities can be assigned to a computer, such as matching of prior student performance with schedule requests or providing simple information. Vocational and career choices can be correlated with the student's past performance and interests. More personal matters —or those not foreseen by the programmer—can be routed to the counselor. Relieving the counselor of some of his information-disseminating role leaves more time for personal relationship between the counselor and student.

Evaluation of CAI Uses

It is important to emphasize that any computer-assisted educational process must be student-centered. Some criteria that may be applied to any proposed educational use of computers should include:

Is unique educational effectiveness demonstrable?

Is there improved efficiency in individual diagnosis and remedial instruction?

Can it be readily integrated with other elements of the educational program?

Does it provide truly individualized instruction or service?

Does it help orient the student to a technological civilization?

Are desirable attitude changes (e.g., increased motivation) produced by CAI?

The stage is set for major breakthroughs in instructional technology and the climate seems ripe in the educational community for increased use of computer-aided instruction. To date, the college has played a leadership role in developing such innovations, with considerable support from the federal government, foundations, and computer manufacturers. But growth toward effective maturity still depends on the support of the broad community of higher education, and such support will probably develop very slowly. The future-oriented administration wisely encourages such interest when it appears but does not try to force history to happen.

TOTAL INFORMATION SYSTEMS

An earlier chapter reviewed the growing number of administrative applications of computers at many colleges. As more and more of these applications develop, it seems that they are sometimes islands and that the seas between them can be very rough. Each administrative department may develop its own system for maintaining the information it needs to do its job, without much regard for the needs of other departments. Each new center of activity develops its own new files and its own way of doing things, and there may be duplication, inconsistency, and inconvenience for anyone who needs information which cuts across departmental boundaries.

This situation has always existed, but somehow the use of computers seems to expose and aggravate it. If six different offices keep student records, six different computer programs may eventually exist which carry the student's name, social security number, and address, and six different programmers may design six different ways to code sex, high school record, or marital or draft status. When the student moves or changes his status in any way, somehow six different changes must be made. Either he must go to six different offices and prepare six different forms, or he will go to one office and make the changes and that office will inform the others. Either it is inconvenient for the student or cumbersome for the clerical staff.

Computer Assistance

The computer makes it possible to design a system which avoids these problems. The term "total system" has come to be used for such an approach. (This term is perhaps misleading, since nothing is ever *total*, short of the universe, but the term has stuck and may as well be used.) The key notions involved are integration, centrality, and uniqueness. The shared or common information of various agencies is integrated into a single file, the file is maintained centrally by and for the whole organization, and, whenever possible, each unique datum will be entered and stored only once.

The president may be either puzzled or wearied by hearing frequent pious references to the desirability of the "total systems approach." The essential objective of this approach is not really to include every possible bit of information about every possible aspect of management—or to keep all such data in a central place or operate on it with one central ensemble of machines. *The "total systems approach" is really characterized by a state of mind*, a set of attitudes and objectives, and a widely shared intention to design each part and phase of the system, whether sequentially or all at once, or whether in the same department or in several, so that it fits neatly and helpfully with every other. The approach also seeks to avoid duplication of developmental effort, to maximize the usefulness of every department's data resources to the benefit of every other administrative and academic sector, and to enable the highest level of administration readily to examine a coherent close-up of any one phase of the administrative system—or of as much of the whole administrative picture as can be made meaningful.

The advantages of such a system are obvious. It is easy to update and maintain such files: response to notification of change is immediate; as soon as a student announces his change of address, it is changed for everyone. Communication is simplified: the alumni file is produced automatically from the file of graduating seniors. The dean who wants information on faculty or students across departments can get it without calling each department head individually. The university administrator who wants space utilization information across schools can find it all in one place.

But probably the most important function the total system serves is to make decision-making easier. It provides data concerning the whole college for use in institutional research and for the needs of the top administration. The concept of the total system has been hailed in industry as an important step in giving management information needed for control and planning. In recent years, colleges have also felt the need for better, longer-range planning. With this need comes a requirement for a better knowledge and understanding, in quantitative terms, of what the college is, has been, and will be.

System Problems

This approach to administrative systems is not without problems; the advantages are not reaped without attendant costs. The emphasis in the approach is on common, shared, or compatible data. Agencies which have maintained their own files have been maintaining them in the optimum form for their own use; when they share a file with others, it may have to be designed to serve them all, but not perhaps in optimum fashion for any given user. Decisions must be made about what information will be kept centrally and in what form it should exist. Some information which was of interest to one dean may be scrapped, because no one else sees any need for it. The numbering system for freshmen used by the admissions office and that used by the student aid office may be incompatible, and one system of file numbering will have to be accepted by both.

Though such a system allows for easy entry and retrieval of information, alteration of the *kinds* of information kept may be extremely difficult in an automated system. If, for instance, an item of information (student's high school, for example) is not allowed for, when the system is in operation it will be difficult to add to it. Hence the study of requirements which precedes system design must be very thorough, with some provision for flexibility when, inevitably, it will be altered and expanded.

The designers, too, must decide how much cooperation is possible or desirable. No system is ever total although totality is a goal of any system. The organization must be seen as a whole and must be able to state clear and workable goals for information flow. Some organizations are too big to be served by a single system because they are too complex and because they are innately pluralistic. One state university considered making its information system part of a statewide information system, but this proved to be out of the question. There was indeed some overlap in fiscal and personnel information, but there was so little overlap in goals, functions, and methods between the university and the rest of the state government that such integration was impractical. It was decided that there would be two systems, with provision for coordination and translatability between them.

No such total system currently exists on any college campus, though some claims are made for "almost total." The concept has been introduced in industrial management and has met with some success; it is safe to predict that such systems will begin to appear in higher education in the next few years. Large universities have been the first to feel the demands for more and faster access to better information. But the need is beginning to be felt at the smaller institution as well. Virtually every college administration now feels that it is in a period of change and that a better understanding of the past and present is needed to chart a future course.

On-line Systems

There is no insuperable technical problem blocking the construction of total systems. Some are in the development stages today. Technical innovations may, however, spell the further development of the information system on campus (as it has in industry) into the real-time, on-line system utilizing the time-shared computer of the research and instructional system. Such systems, using the hardware and software described above, will allow several very positive advantages, specifically current updating of information, query capability, and direct user access.

In a real-time information system, the procedure for introducing new data is simplified. If the student appears at the registrar's office with a change of address, the change is typed on a direct input device by the clerk who deals with the student; before he leaves the office, the change has been made and verified.

The system will allow the user to query the data base in a flexible format at any time. Much of the present cumbersome report-generation will no longer be necessary. Most present-day computer-produced reports are very long and detailed. The available information must be accessible to *any qualified person who wants to see it*. If the consumer of this report has a console on which he can request just that subset of data he needs he will soon realize that the fat compendium is no longer necessary. For example, many presidents see on their desks every month a complete report on the budgetary status of all contracts and grants. This is useful if one wants to learn about how Professor X is doing, but a system which he could at any time interrogate about the status of Professor X's contract frees him from dealing with largely unnecessary reports. Exception reporting will alert him to anything sufficiently anomalous to require attention at once.

The development of on-line systems with relatively convenient languages will bring the user himself closer to the information in the data base. If a report is desired (for example, on faculty salary as a function of age), a programmer must now write a program to retrieve the data and produce the report; a week later it is in the user's hands. If he then realizes that he did not want it only by age, but also by employment date or sex, he has another week to wait. A system which allows him to ask the computer system directly for the information he wants, and which gives it to him in a matter of minutes, provides increased flexibility in the ways he can request information.

The Effect on Administrative Structure

It has seemed clear in industry that the use of real-time management information systems may have a profound effect on the way managers perform their function, and on how the organizational hierarchy works. One study of the use of real-time systems in industry states:

When the rationale of installing computer systems is no longer merely clerical cost reduction, but is aimed at satisfying the information requirements of management, many companies find themselves perforce behaving more and more in a centralized fashion. With the information resources at hand, management is no longer happy with suboptimization at a product line or divisional level, but begins to look meaningfully at what is best from a total company point of view. . . .

The evidence indicates that while formal structural compartments within an organization may be retained for some time yet, the management and staff of the information systems department, reporting directly to the top of the corporate hierarchy, is assuming responsibility for more and more of the operations, tactical decision making, planning, and finally, participation in strategic decisions.[5]

The information system finally becomes a vital and central part of the administrative system, and the top level of administration assumes a much greater knowledge of the affairs of the organization. This need not mean on the campus what it does in industry—that the top officers assume a tighter control. It can mean that they are in a better position to judge present activities in terms of long-range educational goals. What the president does with this information is not a function of the system which provides it but of the methods by which he can effectively guide his college toward those goals.

A vital organization necessarily modifies itself to meet new problems and changes in its environment. The introduction of ways of rapidly obtaining new (and more) information is bound eventually to transform the organization. What is important is that those in a position to control this transformation do so and insure that the emergent organization is one which can solve its problems and adapt to its environment effectively. To paraphrase a familiar military aphorism, the administrative use of a total information system is too important to be left to the information system technician.

Such total systems will not emerge quickly, and the development of any one phase should not be delayed until the whole is ready to run smoothly. But the basic concept underlying the design should be to enable the smooth meshing of each new part into the whole. Even while the ultimate system is only partially on its way to full development, the administrator should now and then be happily surprised by what the system can provide him. In fact, he should insist that this be so. Otherwise, the full value of the investment in the system is not being returned.

[5] Sherman C. Blumenthal, "Management in Real Time," *Data Processing Magazine,* August 1965, pp. 18, 20.

IN OTHER WORDS

COMPUTERS ARE PRESENT on hundreds of American campuses, and their presence is being increasingly felt by the top administration. At least 30 percent of America's colleges and universities now have one or more computers; projections suggest that by 1970 the percentage will exceed 50. The value of these computers on campus is estimated to be $400 million. This figure is growing at the rate of 25 percent—or $100 million—per year. This is particularly impressive if one considers that the cost of computation per task has steadily decreased. No college of any size can for long ignore this trend. Those who plan to continue to live without a computer must do so knowing the economic and educational implications.

The phenomenal growth in computer use, off campus and on, which seems always to exceed even the rashest of estimates, has its roots in the basic generality of these machines. Every new survey reveals new areas of application in instruction and research, in the sciences, in the humanities, and in planning and administration. The only limit to the breadth of the application of computers seems to be the imagination of those who use them.

It has already been demonstrated that the computer is an essential resource in an increasingly large sector of the environment served by higher education. The computer has become an indispensable adjunct of research and of the administration of larger institutions. It is rapidly making its presence felt in instruction, even in the smaller college, both as a tool and as an object of teaching. Because it becomes so interactively linked with the methods and the goals of the institutions it serves, the computer cannot be ignored by the college administrator. The president and his staff must understand the role of the computer in their institution, because they must make decisions about the quality of the educational program, the adequacy of resources for instruction and learning, and the efficiency of administrative operations.

College presidents are aware of the computer on campus; some are enthusiastic, some apathetic, and some deeply concerned, even worried. Here are a few of the typical questions they ask:

What can the president delegate and what must he understand for himself?

How does an administrator make sure that the system being designed for him will satisfy his needs?

Should computers proliferate in several centers as the needs warrant, or should the college maintain one monolithic center?

How can computers help the college with its special problems and its need to plan for future development?

How can one decide how much computing is necessary and how much is luxury? That is, how much computing power is "enough"?

How should the computer center be organized so as to inhibit friction and empire-building and yet encourage intelligent and creative use of the machine?

What can the college afford in the way of computers?

The college president asks his staff; he asks visitors to the campus. Presidents ask one another. It was in the face of such questions that this study was undertaken, in an attempt to enunciate some basic principles which presidents have discovered in seeking answers appropriate to their colleges. By way of conclusion, some of the more important of these principles will be restated here, stripped of the anecdotes, details, and arguments of the preceding chapters.

THE COMPUTER IN THE ORGANIZATION

The place of the computer center in the organization of the college is important because it affects the flow of information, and information is the lifeblood of the organization. Under conditions of limited resources (and it is normal for computing itself to be a limited resource), policies governing the allocation of these resources among user communities is an institutionwide responsibility and cannot be left by design or by default to any one party with a vested interest, especially not to the computer center itself.

Those who conducted the interviews reported in this study observed two phenomena which should be pondered by the president. First, there was a high and positive correlation between the general quality of computer systems and services and the awareness on the part of the president of their importance. (One symptom of this awareness was the response of the president's office when he received a call or letter requesting a visit; if the visitors were scheduled to see the president and/or top members of the administration, the situation observed at the institution was generally quite different from that at which the visitors were shunted only to lower-echelon technicians.) Second, especially in large institutions, the self-evaluations of systems and services increased in cheer and glow the closer one approached the top of the organization; if noises at the lower (user) end were noticeably sadder as one descended the hierarchy, serious problems were likely to be found. Conversely, if dissatisfaction with computer resources and their adequacy was more noticeable at or near the president's level and less so at the user level, this was more often than not a symptom of good long-range thinking and of sound understanding by the top administrator of the significance of the role of the computer. Other observable differences in quality among institutions of comparable size and resources were largely due to historical factors (stage of development), internal politics, and the presence or absence of recalcitrant but powerful key figures in the administration or among the faculty.

CENTRALIZATION

If there is more than one computer and/or more than one major user of computers on the campus, the issue of centralization must be faced. The advantages of centralization are mainly financial and are seen as accruing to the administration. The disadvantages are perceived as mainly technical and are seen as impinging upon the users. If users do not have adequate guarantees of access to the computer, they will engage in political and/or acquisitive activities and struggles for priority. If adequate priorities or guaranteed access to computer time cannot be assured centrally, users will try to get their own facilities and will subvert attempts at centralization. Decentralization is not normally supportable on grounds of economy. However, it may be advisable under certain conditions. If any user's needs perturb the rest of the community, it is to their interest to permit his separation. If money is available specifically and exclusively for a separate purpose, the dedication must be honored. If the user cannot obtain satisfactory service from an official agency, he must fend for himself—and most do.

RANGE OF USE

The computer can provide a wide range of services if used imaginatively. If the computer is not serving a wide circle of users on the campus, there has been a failure of communication or of basic system design. The computer is culturally and intellectually important in all higher education, not just in the obvious hard sciences and technologies. Specifically, computing technology is important because it is:

An aid to efficient and effective administration.

A professional tool in a growing number of fields.

An aid to research.

An object of research.

An aid to instruction and learning.

A model of the robots and automata which will increasingly affect society.

The computer, which has already revolutionized concepts of industrial management, is beginning to affect college administration. Almost every administrative function can benefit from the proper use of automated processes—as has already been demonstrated in one or more institutions.

COST AND PLANNING

The cost of computing is by no means equivalent to the cost of the machinery. Computer personnel may cost as much again. Cost must also include housing, site preparations, personnel, and software; these may be as expensive as the hardware itself. Careful distinctions must be made between initial one-time and continuing costs. As was said earlier in this report, the hard-dollar value of a more effective system (with or without a computer at its heart) is found in the byproducts: improved planning, better justification for budgets, more effective controls, better allocation of scarce resources (i.e., all resources), and the release of the professional staff from clerical drudgeries in favor of more time for thinking about, evaluating, and planning programs.

Computer system development is tantamount to the development of capital facilities, requiring long lead time and careful advance planning. Unlike most capital goods, the value of computer resources is not static but is a function of the continuing effectiveness of their use. Furthermore, the capital represented by software is to a surprising extent cheaply reproducible for use by other institutions. The planning of computer-based systems can be enormously complex and is normally accomplished iteratively. It does not come into being full blown but has a natural life history, with characteristic crises and traumas.

IDENTIFICATION, INVOLVEMENT, AND IMAGINATION

It is of utmost importance for the president to understand that the fact that automated processes are used does not relieve the administrative staff members of any of their primary responsibility for the operational efficiency and effectiveness of the functions they perform. It is still they, and not the computer center or its staff, who are responsible for running the college and its programs. The following two extracts from early portions of the report are repeated here to stress the authors' belief in their importance:

It is extremely important for the administrator to understand this proposition: *The computer never makes decisions. It carries them out.* The *decisions* are made when the system is designed—decisions to gather specified kinds of data from particular sources, to examine alternatives and take appropriate actions, to compare current status against criteria, and to create danger signals when things go wrong.

Even a small college can rarely afford *not* to hire a *full-time* director. If he shares his time between the computer center and an academic appointment, one post or the other will suffer. If his true interest is his teaching and research, he will run the center with his left hand and eventually the center will be left to run itself. It is usually true that an organization that runs itself runs down.

The managers of computer resources must identify primarily with the user communities, within the context of the collective *educational goals of the whole institution.* It is probably no more difficult for the president, and for administrators generally, to understand what they have to know about computers than it is for them to command any other technique which must be understood by an administrator using a manual system. The computer is in some ways simpler and in others more complicated than the administrator may imagine. Technically, it is much simpler. One does not need to be a mathematician or an engineer to understand the important principles of the computer, how it works, and what it can do. What is complex is not the machine itself but the pervasive effect it has on the organization and the society which uses it. These are human consequences, and the effects are on people and organizations. It is these things the administrator can and must understand.

The computer can be the most humanizing machine ever devised; it can also create confusion, misinformation, bad feelings, and deficits. The choice is not up to the machine, nor to the technical people who run it. It is up to the administrator who evokes the educational goals of the organization and who leads those around him to achieve them. *The computer only amplifies and implements decisions made or approved by the president.*

A PROSE GLOSSARY

GLOSSARIES OF TECHNICAL TERMS are very often of little use to the novice since their alphabetic order does not reflect any other logical structure. Attempted here is a glossary arranged in a more or less logical fashion, with an index (pages 194–6) to help the nonserial user find a particular term. If the definition does not shed sufficient light, the context may.

1	A COMPUTER is a machine for performing complex processes on
2	information without manual intervention. ANALOG COMPUTERS
3	perform this function by directly measuring continuous physical
4	quantities such as electrical voltages. The best-known analog com-
5	puter is a slide rule. DIGITAL COMPUTERS represent numerical quan-
6	tities by discrete electrical states which can be manipulated logically
7	and hence arithmetically. Digital computers are sometimes referred
8	to as ELECTRONIC DATA PROCESSING MACHINES, EDP, or PROC-
9	ESSORS. In order to distinguish the actual physical equipment from
10	the programs which extend its usefulness, the former is called
11	HARDWARE.
12	The CENTRAL PROCESSOR UNIT (CPU) or MAIN FRAME is the
13	portion of the computer which performs the calculations and deci-
14	sions; the MEMORY or STORAGE is the part in which the data and
15	programs are stored. The CORE MEMORY is the main memory of most
16	modern machines; it is normally the only memory directly accessible
17	to the CPU. Its name derives from its composition: small ferrite
18	rings called CORES. The computer may have additional memory
19	devices; information is transferred between these and the core
20	memory. The most usual such memories are MAGNETIC DRUMS
21	(spinning cylinders with a magnetizable recording surface) and
22	MAGNETIC DISCS (flat spinning discs with magnetizable surfaces).
23	The capability of memory devices is measured in capacity and
24	speed of access. The STORAGE CAPACITY of a memory is measured

25   in WORDS (also called CELLS or REGISTERS) which are usually of fixed
26   length, consisting of from 12 to 48 bits. This number is called the
27   machine's WORD LENGTH. A BIT (binary digit) is the minimum
28   unit of information storage and has only two possible values.
29   Capacity can also be measured in BYTES, units of six or eight bits,
30   each capable of representing one alphabetic or numeric symbol.
31   ACCESS SPEED of a memory is the time it takes for the processor
32   to obtain a word from memory. Core memory is called RANDOM
33   ACCESS when any word can be obtained at any time without regard to
34   its serial order. Drum, tape, and disc memories are SERIAL ACCESS
35   because the words pass one at a time as they move past the station
36   where they may be accessed. Speed is usually spoken of in terms of
37   MILLISECONDS (m) (thousandths of seconds), MICROSECONDS (μ)
38   (millionths of a second), or NANOSECONDS (n or v) (billionths of
39   a second). One nanosecond is the time required for light to travel
40   almost one foot.
41   The central processor and the memory constitute the computer per
42   se; to get data and programs into the machine and the results out are
43   the role of the INPUT/OUTPUT EQUIPMENT or I/O.
44   INPUT DEVICES convert information to a form in which it can be
45   stored in the computer's memory. The commonest form of input is
46   the PUNCHED CARD or HOLLERITH CARD (after its inventor). Input
47   devices which accept cards are called CARD READERS and the
48   function they perform is commonly called READING, as is that of all
49   input devices. Cards have 80 COLUMNS with 12 possible punch posi-
50   tions; normally, each column is used to represent one character. A set
51   of cards is called a DECK. Another form of input is PUNCHED PAPER
52   TAPE—continuous tape approximately one inch wide, with holes
53   punched across its width to represent characters or numeric quanti-
54   ties. MAGNETIC INK CHARACTER READERS have come to be used for
55   input, particularly in banking; they can interpret characters printed
56   with a special ink. More recently, OPTICAL SCANNERS have appeared,
57   which can read clearly printed or typed material of given type fonts.
58   OUTPUT DEVICES usually include a CARD PUNCH (which converts
59   the characters stored in memory to punched holes in a card), a TAPE
60   PUNCH (which performs the same function for punched paper tape),
61   and a LINE PRINTER (which prints numerals, letters, and other char-
62   acters of conventional design on continuous rolls of paper). Passing

63 information to these devices, the computer is WRITING. Recent addi-
64 tions to the output family include the DISPLAY DEVICE which exhibits
65 readable characters or graphic information on the face of a CATHODE
66 RAY TUBE or CRT. These images must be read at once, of course, since
67 they are not permanent.
68   Information which can be taken away in permanent form (such as
69 the output line printer) is called HARD COPY. A PLOTTER is an output
70 device which, under computer control, can draw continuous lines or
71 curves on paper, thus producing graphs, maps, etc., in hard copy.
72 MAGNETIC TAPE is widely used both as a form of memory and input/
73 output. It can be stored conveniently away from the machine and
74 can be read or written by the computer if it is put on a TAPE DRIVE
75 attached to the computer. It is the fastest type of I/O and the slowest
76 type of memory except when used for serial reading.
77   I/O devices connected directly to the computer memory and
78 under control of the CPU are spoken of as being ON-LINE. They
79 are placed OFF-LINE when they are used to perform independent
80 functions. For example, it is common to exchange information be-
81 tween punched cards and magnetic tape off-line. Some devices are
82 always off-line. They are PERIPHERAL EQUIPMENT and are generally
83 called collectively ELECTROMECHANICAL ACCOUNTING MACHINES
84 or EAM. These are frequently used independent of the computer
85 and in fact antedate computers by many years. The most common
86 are the KEYPUNCH, used to punch cards, the REPRODUCER, which
87 makes copies of decks of cards, and the SORTER, which places cards
88 in different bins as a function of which holes are punched. In some
89 recent systems, another on-line input/output device has been added,
90 the CONSOLE or TERMINAL. These are intended for the user to
91 interact directly with the machine, and usually consist of a type-
92 writer-like keyboard, and either a typewriter-like printing mecha-
93 nism or another display device for output.
94   Information is stored in the computer's memory in the form of
95 the presence or absence of a magnetic charge. A collection of such
96 "yes or no" physical states is usually thought of as a BINARY NUM-
97 BER (a number whose only possible digits are 0 and 1). Depending
98 on context, such numbers can have many meanings; in this sense,
99 the numbers are CODED. They can be interpreted as numeric quanti-
100 ties, CHARACTERS (letters, digits, punctuation marks) or as IN-

101   STRUCTIONS or COMMANDS which will direct the computer to per-
102   form its basic functions (add, compare, read, etc.).
103   A set of instructions to perform a specified function or solve a
104   complete problem is called a PROGRAM. The computer performs
105   such instructions sequentially. However, as the computer can
106   modify the data in its memory, it can also modify its program.
107   This capability to modify its own directions is a case of the engi-
108   neering principle called FEEDBACK, the modification of future per-
109   formance on the basis of past performance. It is because of this
110   distinctive feature that modern digital computers are sometimes
111   called STORED-PROGRAM COMPUTERS. Parts of programs are some-
112   times called ROUTINES or SUBROUTINES. Subroutines which per-
113   form generally useful functions are sometimes combined into a
114   subroutine LIBRARY, usually on magnetic tape. Copies of relevant
115   subroutines will be added to a program automatically and hence
116   need not be developed by hand. Single instructions in a program
117   are sometimes called STEPS. When a sequence of program steps is
118   operated repeatedly, the process is called a LOOP. Certain instruc-
119   tions compare two quantities and select either of two program
120   paths on the basis of the result: these are called BRANCHING in-
121   structions.
122   The data on which a program acts are usually structured into
123   TABLES. Individual values which control the operation of programs
124   or subroutines are PARAMETERS. An organized collection of infor-
125   mation in the computer or on tape is called a FILE, like the or-
126   ganized set of papers in a file cabinet. A DATA BASE or DATA BANK
127   is a large and complex set of tables which describe some aspect
128   of the world outside of the computer (a library catalog, a student
129   record file, a budget).
130   A PROGRAMMER is a person who converts a problem into a set
131   of directions to a computer to solve it. The function is sometimes
132   broken down into several parts, particularly if the problem is very
133   complex. The task of stating the problem in a clear and unambigu-
134   ous form is performed by an ANALYST or SYSTEM ANALYST. The
135   technique of specifying methods of solution for mathematical prob-
136   lems is MATHEMATICAL ANALYSIS or NUMERICAL ANALYSIS. A
137   specific procedure for solving a problem is an ALGORITHM. The
138   process of writing the detailed step-by-step instructions for the
139   computer to follow is CODING done by a CODER.

140   After a program is written, it is tested by letting it perform its
141   function in the computer on test data to which the proper solution
142   is known. This process is CODE-CHECKING or DEBUGGING. The coder
143   will also produce some descriptions of this program and how it
144   operates so that others may understand how it works, in case at a
145   future date, it is necessary to modify it. This DOCUMENTATION
146   may include a FLOW CHART: a graphic description or diagram of
147   the various paths and branches followed by the program.
148   The repertory of instructions available to the programmer for a
149   specific computer is that computer's MACHINE LANGUAGE. Other
150   HIGHER-ORDER LANGUAGES have been developed to help the pro-
151   grammer by simplifying the tedious aspects of writing machine
152   language; these are called PROCEDURE-ORIENTED LANGUAGES or
153   PROBLEM-ORIENTED LANGUAGES or POL. Commonly used POL's
154   are FORTRAN, ALGOL, and COBOL; the first two were devised
155   mainly for scientific computation and the latter for business data
156   processing. A new type is represented by LIST-PROCESSING LAN-
157   GUAGES; because of greater flexibilities in dealing with data, these
158   languages are particularly useful in nonnumeric computations such
159   as are frequently involved in research. Their particular virtues are
160   most apparent in HEURISTIC PROCESSES: methods where the precise
161   method of solution is not spelled out but is discovered as the pro-
162   gram progresses and as it evaluates its progress toward an ac-
163   ceptable solution. (Because this use of the word "language" is
164   somewhat misleading, human languages such as English are dis-
165   tinguished as NATURAL LANGUAGES.)
166   Programs which convert higher-order languages into machine
167   language are called COMPILERS; programs which perform similar
168   functions but at a much simpler level are ASSEMBLERS. The term
169   TRANSLATOR is used sometimes for compiler, but it is used less
170   frequently because of the possible confusion with programs which
171   perform translation between natural languages. INTERPRETERS do not
172   compile the entire program but translate and perform one statement
173   of the program at a time; effectively, they perform both functions
174   —compiling and running a program.
175   SOFTWARE is the term used to refer to the totality of programs
176   and procedures available on a computer; sometimes it is used more
177   specifically to mean those programs of general usefulness (such as
178   compilers) which are available to all users. These are sometimes

179 called UTILITY PROGRAMS. All machines today have OPERATING
180 SYSTEMS to aid the user (and the operator) in sequencing jobs,
181 accounting, and calling up other utility programs. Operating sys-
182 tems or programs are also called CONTROL PROGRAMS, SUPERVISORS,
183 or EXECUTIVES.

184   APPLICATIONS are the problems to which a computer is ap-
185 plied; the names for most common applications are self-explanatory,
186 but some are not. A SIMULATION is the representation of a real
187 or hypothetical system by a computer process; its function is to
188 indicate system performance under various conditions by program
189 performance. INFORMATION RETRIEVAL is the name applied to
190 processes which recover or locate information in a collection of
191 documents. An INFORMATION MANAGEMENT SYSTEM helps a user
192 maintain a data base, modify it, and get reports from it. It is
193 usually defined as a GENERAL-PURPOSE DEVICE; this means that it
194 can accommodate a large range of applications. A MANAGEMENT
195 INFORMATION SYSTEM supplies to the management of an organiza-
196 tion the data that it requires to make decisions and to exercise
197 control. A REPORT GENERATOR is a program which allows the user
198 to specify in some simple way the content and format of reports
199 which the computer is to produce.

200   To RUN a program is to cause it to be performed on the com-
201 puter. Running a program to solve a problem or produce real re-
202 sults (as opposed to debugging) is called a PRODUCTION RUN.
203 Installations in which the user runs his own job are called OPEN
204 SHOPS. Installations which have a COMPUTER OPERATOR who runs
205 the programs for the user are CLOSED SHOPS. Computers are usually
206 operated in BATCH-PROCESSING MODE; the operator assembles a
207 batch of programs waiting to be run and puts them serially into
208 the computer; output from all the programs is returned in one
209 batch. TURNAROUND TIME is the time between the user's delivering
210 his job to the center and his receipt of his output. TIME-SHARING
211 is a method of operation by means of which several jobs are inter-
212 leaved, giving the appearance of simultaneous operation. In many
213 time-shared systems, users have individual terminals which are on-
214 line. Such terminals may be located far from the computer; this is
215 REMOTE ACCESS. This allows users to interact with the computer on
216 a time scale appropriate for human beings—on the order of a few
217 seconds between responses. This capability is called operating in

218 REAL TIME. Using the computer for frequent interaction with the
219 user in this way is called an INTERACTIVE or CONVERSATIONAL mode
220 of computing.
221   Like all electronic devices, computers sometimes break down.
222 The prevention and correction of such situations is MAINTENANCE.
223 PREVENTIVE MAINTENANCE finds failing components before they
224 actually break down. RELIABILITY is the measure of the frequency
225 of failure of the computer. During DOWN-TIME the machine is
226 being maintained or repaired; during UP-TIME it is available for
227 normal productive use.   C. J. M.

GLOSSARY INDEX

APPENDIX

Author's Note: As was mentioned in the text, the American Association of Collegiate Registrars and Admissions Officers (AACRAO) has conducted several annual surveys of the use of computers by its members and their institutions in connection with student admissions and records. This survey was repeated in December 1966 and provides some of the most up-to-date information in this special but not untypical field. The data were compiled from 1,361 institutions of higher education by the New Developments and Techniques Committee of AACRAO's Data Systems and Machine Activities Group. AACRAO has graciously given permission to summarize here some of the data which should be of considerable interest to administrators assessing the impact and diffusion of computer-aided administrative systems. Additional information about the survey, which has been published for AACRAO members, may be obtained from the Executive Secretary of AACRAO (1501 New Hampshire Avenue, N.W., Washington, D.C. 20036) or from William E. Slaby, Registrar, Wayne State University, Detroit.

THE 1966-67 SURVEY is prefaced by a very helpful "Analysis of Trends in Computer Usage," written by Reverend Orrin Wheeler, Xavier University, Cincinnati. Though the AACRAO survey would not normally have revealed administrative data systems which had no connection with AACRAO's concerns, the results show how rapidly and widely the computer has been adopted as an administrative resource in higher education.

Table A indicates the relationship between use of computers and institional size.

The administrative responsibility for providing AACRAO-related services is the subject of the report's Table B, which also shows the relationship of such placement to enrollment category. Since Table B shows more detail than the average reader may care to know, the findings are summarized as follows: Fewer than 4 percent of institutions place responsibility in the admissions or registrar's office! Fewer than 8 percent place this operation in the business office, and fewer than 10 percent place it in some other department. The most frequent (modal) practice (30.8 percent) is to place the operation in a combined academic, research, and administrative center. The next most frequent (28.4 percent) location is in a cen-

TABLE A

ENROLLMENT	INSTALLATIONS		
RANGE	Using Computer	Not Using	TOTAL
Under 1,000	62	476	538
1,000-5,000	257	320	577
5,000-10,000	135	18	153
Over 10,000	125	6	131
Size unknown	6	7	13
TOTALS	585	827	1,412

Comments. Two out of every five of the 1,412 installations use a computer for admissions and/or pupil records. Three out of every five institutions with an enrollment over 1,000 use computers, and more than nine out of every ten institutions over 5,000 in enrollment use them.

tralized administrative unit. Hence about three out of every five institutions put the responsibility in either a general-purpose administrative unit or in a combined academic-administrative unit. The use of a commercial outside agency or neighboring institution is reported in fewer than 20 percent of institutions, but with a strong tendency for small (enrollment under 1,000) institutions to make such an arrangement. The AACRAO trend data show a marked jump in the past year in the use of external agencies or centers.

Table C of the AACRAO report presents statistics on the various kinds of applications for which computers were used, again by enrollment size and again at a level of detail which seems inappropriate for our report. The original report should be consulted by those interested in such details. This table reports not only the number making a particular application but also what relative proportion of the center's work is devoted to each. Only in the smallest institutions does enrollment size seem to have a frequent bearing on the occurrence or preponderance of utilization.

Ignoring institutional size, the AACRAO report's Table C shows that the most frequent applications (in more than one-half of those reporting) are generating grade reports, posting to permanent records, institutional research, scholastic actions (probation, honors), and enrollment studies— in that order. Uses so infrequent as to be eliminated from the table this year included generating individual transcripts, financial aid operations, partial or complete degree auditing, and the construction of master schedules. It is worth noting that more than one-half of the large (over 5,000) institutions reported using computers to assemble and analyze data in the admissions process.

The body of the *AACRAO Survey Report* lists each responding institution, by state, with many details about equipment, administration, and utilization. Those evaluating their own patterns of use relative to what others of their own size, type, or region are doing, will find the report helpful. At the end of the report results are summarized by state, and there are few surprises—larger and more affluent states being the biggest users. This final table, however, shows some interesting trends. Of those not now having a computer, almost one hundred indicate that one is on order, and about sixty others report that there is a computer on campus which they are not now using. In addition, many institutions report that they are programming new applications which are not yet in operation. The latter is most likely to be true in smaller institutions.   J.C.

BIBLIOGRAPHY

Some readers may wish to know more about some aspects of the subjects discussed in this book. Fortunately some good books and articles are available for further reading. It is no longer true, as it once was, that anything published about computers was necessarily already out-of-date. Our intent is not to cover the field but to present a few references which have stood the test of the expert, who finds them accurate, and the novice, who finds them generally clear and meaningful.

THE COMPUTER

There are a number of good books which explain what computers are and what they do. Many of these are textbooks, however, and include too much detail or technical material. Two which are clearly not in this category but are intended to introduce the computer to the armchair reader are Jeremy Bernstein, *The Analytical Engine* (New York: Random House, 1964) and D. S. Haldacy, Jr., *Computers—The Machines We Think With* (New York: Harper & Row, 1962). Bernstein's book is a lucid and engaging introduction to computers—their history, their operations, their implications—by a man who is a physicist and also a staff writer for *The New Yorker*. Haldacy's book is also thorough and unpedantic. It has one valuable asset which Bernstein's book lacks—numerous illustrations.

Although directed at industrial managers, large portions of Paul T. Smith, *How to Live with Your Computer* (New York: American Management Association, 1965), subtitled "A Nontechnical Guide for Managers," will be interesting to and appropriate for academic administrators.

The brief collection of essays in Herbert A. Simon, *The Shape of Automation* (New York: Harper & Row, 1965), is one of the finest discussions of the broad implications of computers and automation that we have seen. It explores, primarily in the context of administration, what computers can be expected to do and their role in decision-making.

Computer Characteristics Quarterly (Cambridge, Mass.: Charles W. Adams Associates) lists all of the commercially available computers, made by a variety of vendors, with a tabular description of their most important features. It exhibits dramatically the broad range of computers available for lease or purchase.

APPLICATIONS

The reader may be interested in looking at one book in a field which parallels his own academic interests. It will give him an idea of the amount of effort going into computer-assisted academic research and the extent of sophistication of some of the user communities. Among these are: Dell Hymes, ed., *The Use of Computers in Anthropology* (London: Monton, 1965); Bert F. Green, *Digital Computers in Research: An Introduction for Behavioral and Social Scientists* (New York: McGraw-Hill Book Co., 1963); Theodor D. Sterling and Seymour V. Pollack, *Computers and the Life Sciences* (New York: Columbia University Press, 1965); Harold Borko, *Computer Applications in the Behavioral Sciences* (Englewood Cliffs, N.J.: Prentice-Hall, 1962); Paul Wasserman, *The Librarian and the Machine* (Detroit: Gale Research Co., 1965); and John M. Fowler, *The Computer in Physics Instruction* (Irvine, Calif.: Commission on College Physics, 1966). The Fowler monograph, though aimed at a single field, is extremely helpful in that it explains general features of computers which will enlighten the reader interested in their instructional uses. The Hymes volume is a large collection of papers from several nations and is of very great general interest because it contains descriptions and examples of a variety of techniques which are helpful in many different fields of scholarly research, including the hard sciences.

THE COMPUTER AND HIGHER EDUCATION

There are a few works in the general field of computers and the college which can be recommended. There is also, of course, a wealth of detailed material on specific applications. Anyone who doubts the fact that the computer has a role in college administration should look, for example, at any of the proceedings of the College and University Machine Records Conference (available through the Educational Systems Corp., P.O. Box 3711, Georgetown Station, Washington, D.C. 20007).

Usually called the "Rosser Report," *Digital Computer Needs in Universities and Colleges* (Washington: Committee on Uses of Computers, National Academy of Sciences, 1966) contains a wealth of facts, now moderately outdated, and statistics and projections on the computer on campus.

The most recent and possibly most signficant statement about the role of *Computers in Higher Education* (Washington, D.C.: The White

House, 1967) is the report issued by the President's Science Advisory Committee. The committee's special panel on computers lists ten significant findings, each accompanied by a specific recommendation for action on the part of colleges and universities and/or public agencies. The background materials and data accompanying and supporting the panel's findings provide a succinct, readable, and timely summary of recent developments and new directions. This 79-page pamphlet includes very valuable illustrations, statistics, and arguments to support the position of the administrator who wishes to make or keep his academic computing resources adequate to current and predictable needs. The report is available from the Superintendent of Documents, United States Government Printing Office, for 30 cents.

Francis E. Rourke and Glenn E. Brooks, *The Managerial Revolution in Higher Education* (Baltimore: The Johns Hopkins Press, 1966) is an excellent and very up-to-date study of some of the innovations in academic administration, including institutional research and new methods of resource allocation. Chapter 2, "The Computerized Campus," is of special interest, containing normative data on computer applications, gathered from a special survey.

Two booklets which will be found particularly useful to the institution planning its first move into computers are Southern Regional Education Board, *Guidelines for Planning for Computer Centers in Universities and Colleges* (Atlanta: SREB, 1963) and J. W. Hamblen and W. F. Atchison, *Cooperative Planning Computer and Computer Science Programs in Higher Education* (Atlanta: Southern Regional Education Board, 1966).

A broad range of topics is covered in the reprint in book form of the September 1966 issue of *Scientific American, A Scientific American Book of Information* (New York: Scientific American, 1966). Although the articles go into some depth, they are profusely and helpfully illustrated and are written for the intelligent nonspecialist. A broad range of topics is covered; of particular interest are Patrick Suppes' discussion of computers in education and Martin Greenberger's paper on administrative uses of computers.

Harry Williams, *Planning for Effective Resource Allocation in Universities* (Washington: American Council on Education, 1966) explains in simple terms the concepts of "program budgeting," a useful technique for exploiting a computerized financial accounting system, also treated by Rourke and Brooks in the book cited above. The work of Richard W. Judy and Jack B. Levine, *A New Tool for Educational Administrators* (Toronto: University of Toronto Press, 1965) provides an excellent description of the use of simulation as an administrative tool.

THE FUTURE

Books predicting what the future is going to look like generally make very poor reading, unless they admit to being science fiction. J. C. R. Licklider, *Libraries of the Future* (Cambridge, Mass.: The M.I.T. Press, 1965) may read like science fiction but it bases itself firmly in fact. It gives a mind-stretching picture of the future of the research library as the intellectual heart of the university. A number of interesting papers appears in Martin Greenberger, ed., *Computers and the World of the Future* (Cambridge, Mass.: The M.I.T. Press, 1962). "The Computer in the University" by Alan J. Perlis is particularly recommended.

The AACRAO annual surveys, *Electronic Data Processing Survey Report* (Knoxville: American Association of Collegiate Registrars and Admissions Officers), provides valuable and typical normative data on equipment, administrative placement, and types of applications. The 1966-67 survey shows that 585 out of 1,361 institutions polled were using computers for one or more phases of admissions and student records. The section on "Analysis of Trends" will be especially interesting and significant to the administrator looking toward the future.

PERIODICALS

There are many professional and commercial periodicals which deal with general and special aspects of computer technology, and several occasionally contain articles about educational applications. Two are slanted directly at the world of education. The *Journal of Educational Data Processing* (P.O. Box 3711, Georgetown Station, Washington, D.C. 20007)—The Fall 1966 issue of the *Journal*, available in single copies, was devoted entirely to problems of college and university information systems —and *AEDS Monitor* (Association for Educational Data Systems, 1201 16th Street, N.W., Washington, D.C. 20036). AEDS maintains a useful information center at the address given.

Many administrative applications not limited to business management are treated in two commercial periodicals: *College Management* (22 West Putnam Ave., Greenwich, Conn. 06830) and *College and University Business* (1050 Merchandise Mart, Chicago, Ill. 60654). The March 1967 issue of *College Management* reports a census of computers in American colleges and universities—one of the most ambitious and comprehensive undertaken to date.

An "Automation Educator" supplement is included several times a year in *Business Automation* (228 Park Ave., West, Elmhurst, Ill. 60126).

INDEX

Note: Some terms, especially technical ones, are used so ubiquitously in the text that specific citations are impractical or not helpful. If such a word is not listed in this index, or if only a definition is needed, consult the *Glossary* and *Glossary Index*, pp. 187-96.

accessibility 9, 27-33 *passim*, 117-9, 119-21, 125-7, 127-47 *passim*
accessibility of information 17, 36
   see also data base (bank); information management; information retrieval
accounting 52-7
accounts 6
   integrated 53-7
acquisition, computer 81-2, 83-4, 92-5, 96-110 *passim*
   see also decisions, presidential; planning for computer uses
acquisition, personnel 9, 96, 135-7
administrative applications 6-7, 34-51, 52-67, 179, 182
   see also managerial uses; transactional uses
administrative systems 17-8, 18-20, 40, 56, 63
admissions 34, 41-3, 61
allocations *see* resources allocation
applications, analysis of 101-3, 128, 132-3, 159-77
attitudes 103-5, 105-9, 117-9, 137, 142-5, 183-4
auxiliary enterprises 53

backup 94
batch-processing 28-33, 154-5
billing 34, 40, 41, 44, 53
budgets 6, 52, 53, 56-7, 64
buffering 31

capabilities 16, 18-20, 23, 40-3, 148-57 *passim*, 159-77 *passim*
capacity 21, 149-51
centralization 112, 174-7, 181
   versus decentralization 117-21
character sets 151-3
charges 137-42
closed shop 28
   see also modes of operations
COBOL 24, 104, 155
committee, selection *see* task force
committee, users' 113, 114-6

compatibility 94, 100, 101, 120-4, 179, 182
compiler(s) 24-5, 73-4, 93
   see also languages, computer
components 20-3
computer science 69, 74, 77, 73-9 *passim*, 118, 170-1
computers
   defined 1, 14-8 *passim*, 20-5 *passim*
   in general education 77-80, 156-7
   generations of 18
   as professional tool 69, 156-7
   research in 73-5, 148-57 *passim*, 159-77
consultants 97, 133
control of computing resources 4-6, 8, 111-2, 117-9
   see also attitudes; management of facilities
control purposes 7, 19, 35, 53, 57, 65
conversational mode 152-4
cooperation, interinstitutional 121-4
costing 137-42
   direct 139-40
   indirect 138-9
costs 9, 21, 24, 25, 29, 37-8, 56, 85-9, 92-3, 95, 111, 119-23, 137-42, 149-51, 169-70, 182-3
counseling 36, 43, 45-6, 171-2
CRT displays 152-4, 165-6, 167-8
curriculum 76-80, 170-1

data analysis (reduction) 70, 71
data base (bank) 6-7, 7, 34-5, 43, 34-50 *passim*, 54, 59, 63-4, 52-67 *passim*, 155, 174-7
decision-making 7, 45, 59-63, 64, 65, 172-7, 179-80, 183-4
decisions, presidential 3, 81, 97, 102-3, 179-81
   see also decision-making; management of facilities; planning for computer use
delegation *see* decision-making
design, system 2, 34-5, 55, 96, 102-3, 108, 109, 174-7

AMERICAN COUNCIL ON EDUCATION

Logan Wilson, President

The American Council on Education, founded in 1918, is a *council* of educational organizations and institutions. Its purpose is to advance education and educational methods through comprehensive voluntary and cooperative action on the part of American educational associations, organizations, and institutions.

Date Due

Due	Returned	Due	Return
NOV 18 1992	NOV 04 1992		
FEB 05 1993	FEB 05 1993		
MAR 29 1993	APR 11 1993		